TEACHERS' EVERYDAY USE
OF IMAGINATION
AND INTUITION

SUNY SERIES,
TEACHER PREPARATION AND DEVELOPMENT

ALAN R. TOM, EDITOR

TEACHERS' EVERYDAY USE
OF IMAGINATION AND INTUITION

IN PURSUIT
OF THE ELUSIVE IMAGE

VIRGINIA M. JAGLA

STATE UNIVERSITY OF NEW YORK PRESS

Published by
State University of New York Press, Albany

Printed in the United States of America

For information, address State University of New York
Press, State University Plaza, Albany, N.Y., 12246

Product by Diane Ganeles
Marketing by Theresa Abad Swierzowski

Library of Congress Cataloging-in-Publication Data

Jagla, Virginia M., 1948-
    Teachers' everyday use of imagination and intuition : in pursuit
of the elusive image / Virginia M. Jagla.
        p.   cm. — (SUNY series, teacher preparation and development)
    Includes bibliographical references (p.   ) and index.
    ISBN 0-7914-2097-3 (alk. paper). — ISBN 0-7914-2098-1 (pbk. :
alk. paper)
    1. Teachers. 2. Teaching. 3. Imagination. 4. Intuition
(Psychology) 5. Classroom management. I. Title. II. Series: SUNY
series in teacher preparation and development.
LB1025.3.J34 1994
371.1—dc20   93-42684
                                                                          CIP

10 9 8 7 6 5 4 3 2 1

For my loving husband, Jeff,
and our darling daughter, Frances.

CONTENTS

PART I

INITIAL IMAGES

What images does the word **teacher** conjure up for you? What do you think of when you hear the word **educate**? How do you picture a school? What is the best environment for learning?

We each have our own conceptions about various aspects of education depending on our backgrounds. Often the teachers we have had and schools we have attended color our impressions to a great extent. Depending on your personal experience in the field of education, your ideas might deviate from your own school days to more current experiences.

How important is it for teachers to utilize their own imaginations and intuition while engaged in the process of educating? How might this occur? How do **you** use your imagination in teaching? Are you intuitive? Does it make any sense to explore such esoteric ideas?

In this first part of the book, I will frame some introductory context for these rather enigmatic phenomena and contemplate images of "artistic teachers" as painted by various authors and teachers themselves. Come explore teachers' everyday use of imagination and intuition.

CHAPTER 1

INTRODUCTION

Lead me from darkness to light!
> —Brihadaranyaka Upanishad

I shall light a candle of understanding in thine heart, which shall not be put out.
> —The Apocrypha

Is education really possible in schools? To educate, *educare*, originally meant to lead out—specifically to lead one from darkness into the light. The ancient Indian word for teacher, *guru*, means the one who shows the way from darkness into light (gu = darkness; ru = light). **Who is able "to educate"? to enlighten? Have we lost sight of the true meaning of teaching? Is the teaching process merely a training procedure?**

Even with the onslaught of school reform and much needed attention being given to improvement and "restructuring" of the education process in general, the ever popular method of teaching in many public schools remains a relatively rigid, formal approach to the basics. Subject matter is still most often taught in inflexible blocks. Facts and skills are further isolated to be memorized and learned in a somewhat stifling and often boring manner. **Is this education? Can enlightenment actually occur in a school setting?** Almost a century ago John Dewey championed the idea that schooling need not be so tedious. Dewey (1900 and 1902) depicted the "old education" as a result of distorted ideas about learning and teaching. Dewey (1938) argued for experiential learning, replacing drill and practice with spontaneous discovery and excitement.

The lack of adventure and excitement in so many schools is a problem today as it was in Dewey's time. The Progressive school movement of the early 1900s did not have the profound effect that many in the movement had hoped. Many bandwagons passed by to turn the heads of the masses. The current "Back to Basics" banners are waving high and catching the eyes of many. The trend implies efficiency with regard to time and effort. Many school systems are looking for the most "bang for the buck." It is important to demonstrate as much "growth" as possible for each dollar spent. Such "growth" is most often measured by an increased gain on annual test scores.

There is no doubt that relevant, imaginative learning and teaching require a great deal of self-investment on the part of all concerned. Followers of Dewey had no idea how hard it would be to teach as he wished. Dewey, himself, confirmed this manner of teaching as arduous (Edwards 1966). Yet there are many teachers who tirelessly invest themselves with their classes year after year to make learning exciting and meaningful.

The Deweyan philosophy lives in the hearts and minds of many educators and is practiced in schools today by those who know the joy of learning. This concept of teaching implies the need for teachers' use of their own imaginative capacities while interacting with students to engage them in truly enjoyable and relevant learning.

What is so special about these good teachers who evoke such charged and excited responses from their students?

There is much research focusing on the teacher as the pivotal entity within the educative process. Teacher thinking research and studies of teacher knowledge comprise a wide body of provocative literature (Brophy and Rohrkemper 1981; Clandinin 1986; Clark and Peterson 1986; Connelly and Ben-Peretz 1980; Elbaz 1983; Finch 1978; Garcia 1987; Goodlad and Klein 1970; Haley-Oliphant 1987; Jackson 1968; Janesick 1982; Marcelo 1987; Richards and Gipe 1988; Richert 1987; Russell and Johnston 1988; Seidman and Santilli 1988).

Freema Elbaz (1983) assumes that "teachers hold a complex, practically-oriented set of understandings which they use actively to shape and direct the work of teaching" (p. 3). D. Jean Clandinin (1986) feels that the experiences of teachers and the images that teachers hold of these experiences offer important contributions to the field of educational research. In her opinion it is paramount that the teachers' perspectives take precedence over the view of the researcher. It makes a lot of sense to look at what "good" teachers do and to ascertain how they do it in order to improve the profession in general.

I became interested in focusing on a specific type of teacher thinking and knowledge. I examined teachers' use of imagination and intuition in daily classroom activities. I explored the practical knowledge of teachers who have been recognized for excellence.

The specifics of imagination and intuition have been studied with regard to how teachers can foster these modes in students (Barell 1980; De Mille 1976; Feldhusen, Treffinger, and Bahlke 1970; Meyers and Torrance 1965; Noddings and Shore 1984; Sinatra and Stahl-Gemake 1983; Smith 1966; Sutherland 1971; Torrance 1964; Torrance 1981; Torrance and Meyers 1970;

Vaughan 1979). Yet little research exists which explores the practical role that the teacher's imagination and intuition play in the everyday planning and implementation of classroom activities.

While I am continually interested in different ways to expand students' imaginations and tap into their intuitive abilities, I am going to focus more on the ways that teachers themselves utilize these modes when involved with this complex task we call "educating." I studied eight teachers who were recognized for excellence through awards and recommendations (Jagla 1989). The teachers ranged in amount of experience from two years to thirty years. Two were high school teachers, one a college teacher and the others were elementary teachers of primary, intermediate, and junior high. The teachers taught in urban and suburban settings. I interviewed each teacher extensively and observed them in their classrooms. Each interview was recorded and transcribed.

The interviews were guided by major questions and ideas, however, they were loosely structured in an exploratory style (Lincoln and Guba 1985). This style of interviewing encouraged the teachers to determine the relevant aspects that needed to be brought out. Some broad-based questions were used as guides, however, the probing questions that occurred throughout the interview were equally important. Such probes were based on each teacher's input. Some of the guide questions included:

> What does imagination mean to you? What is meant by imaginative teaching?
>
> What does intuition mean to you? How do teachers use intuition when working with a class?
>
> What links do you see between the use of one's imagination and intuition? In what ways are a teacher's use of imagination and intuition in daily classroom activities linked?

How do you use imagination in your daily classroom activities?

What have been some of your most imaginative teaching moments? What was it that made these moments imaginative? What role did intuition play in these imaginative moments?

How do you use imagination in planning and implementing curriculum?

Is being resourceful similar to being imaginative?

How do different student groups affect your use of imagination?

Do particular subjects lend themselves to more imaginative teaching?

How important is it to put things "into context" for students? Is this being imaginative?

In what sense is "interaction" (among people, ideas and/or the environment) important to imagination and intuition?

Are imaginative teachers necessarily intuitive?

Are intuitive teachers necessarily imaginative?

Do you feel that you are more imaginative or more intuitive in your daily classroom activities?

Has your use of imagination and intuition changed as you have gained more confidence with experience?

How can the use of imagination and intuition be fostered through inservice and preservice teacher education?

The interviews were the beginning step toward a dialogue with each teacher. The interviews were conducted with much care and respect for the valued time and commitment each teacher made to this process. This pivotal point was a time for dialogue and free-flowing conversation. This allowed both myself and the other

teacher involved a time to jointly reflect on the phenomena in question and deepen our understanding of our
own thoughts on the matter. We collaborated on interpretation and representation so as to remain true to the
intended meanings. I came to the interviews having
already begun the conversation process with myself. The
teachers came to the interview in the midst of some
related conversation. This "conversation" in the wider
perspective had begun without us and will continue even
though the encounters, for the purpose of this study,
have concluded (Carson 1986). We entered into a particular segment of what Michael Oakeshott (1959) has
called "the conversation of mankind."

The observation time was prearranged. I spent the
whole day as a participant observer in the classroom of
most of the teachers. By availing myself to the classroom setting I was able to analyze "actions-in-context"
(Garfinkel 1977) to aid reflexive understanding of common situations for the teacher. It has been argued
(Garfinkel 1977) that everyday occurrences will be looked
at in a new light when observed by another. This way I
was able to call attention to the teachers' various relevant commonplace activities. ". . . on each occasion that
an account of common activities is used, that they be
recognized for 'another first time' . . ." (Garfinkel 1977, p.
247).

In essence, the day's visit not only gave me a better
situational understanding of the phenomena being questioned, it also encouraged the teacher to reflect on the
questions in a new light. This lead to a common ground
of understanding. This heightened awareness on the part
of the teachers, the increased situational understanding on my part, and the common ground of understanding shared by the teachers and myself were all afforded
through this important step.

I gave a copy of the transcript of the initial interview and a copy of my observational notes to each

teacher for further input. The teachers were given a chance to peruse the data and reflect on any new insights, meanings, understandings, and answers regarding the phenomena being questioned.

> *Mirrors should reflect a little before throwing back images.*
>
> —Jean Cocteau in Des Beaux-Arts

Another collaborative meeting was then scheduled. This session was one-on-one as with the initial interview. I do not like to refer to this session as an interview since its intent was to be nondirective and unstructured. This last encounter was simply a "conversation" with each other, an open-ended time to allow for free-flowing discussion of the phenomena, emergent themes, metaphorical analogies, interpretations and whatever came to mind. Terrance Carson (1986) views the conversation itself as a "mode of doing research." As was the case with the initial interview, the conversation was tape recorded and later transcribed to aid in analysis.

After the transcriptions were completed and copies sent to the respective teachers, I took each transcription and thoroughly combed through it to cull out pertinent aspects. At this time I made initial attempts to place these remarks into categories. These revised versions of each transcript were sent to the respective teachers for their further perusal and approval. A few teachers made only minor corrections, while others reflected further and reworded entire sections. It is from these revised transcripts that all teachers' quotes have been selected.

I include myself in the process. My own experiences as an elementary and junior high teacher originally sparked my interest into teachers' use of imagination and intuition. My experience as a college teacher and as an administrator in school districts has given me further insight. At one point, I actually sat down at the word processor and "interviewed" myself. That is, I reflected on some of the questions that I had been asking the teachers in the study. These notes have been woven together with the other teachers' words.

Organization of the Book

Literature that portrays Images of Artistic Teachers is considered here in Part I. "Artistic teachers" (Rubin 1985), exemplary in their art have much to offer, not only to their immediate students, but to the broader educational community in general. Imagination and intuition have been found to play significant roles in the daily operation of "artistic" teachers' classrooms. The metaphor of teaching as art has bearing on the overall topic.

The terms imagination and intuition are examined in Part II: Expressions of Imagination and Intuition. In the Definition of Terms chapter, imagination and intuition are defined historically, colloquially and in reference to particular teachers. The Further Understanding in Context chapter provides meaning which is deeply embedded in the teachers' everyday use of imagination and intuition. Teachers' own recounting of examples in story form are an attempt to surface this embedded meaning.

In Part III: Thematic Threads Unraveled, some of the threads of understanding that weave through the phenomena of teachers' everyday use of imagination and intuition are examined. Many themes are examined separately to enhance the comprehension of the complex elements involved. The ultimate purpose for isolating some of these "threads" or ideas for scrutiny is to enhance meaningful understanding of the phenomena in question. Often by breaking down a complex concept and examining more comprehensible portions, the ultimate understanding of the phenomenon is increased. In chapter 5, Free to Be, I explore the idea of freedom in education as it relates to "Spontaneity and Openness," "Confidence and Experience," and "Familiarity." Chapter 6, Compare and Contrast, looks at the similarities and differences found in the ideas woven throughout discussions of teachers' use of imagination and intuition as they relate to "Particular Subjects or Groups," "Resourcefulness," "Variation and Possibilities," "Randomness versus Structure" and "Intuition and Imagination—Necessarily Wedded?". I envision how The Classroom Comes Alive in chapter 7 by pondering the themes of "Interaction," "Connections and Context," "Storytelling" and "Emotion—Excitement, Love and Caring."

Chapter 8, Cultivating Teachers' Use of Imagination and Intuition, in Part IV explores ways of fostering imagination and intuition with teachers. Since I highly value teachers' use of their own imaginations and intuition when teaching, it is logical for me to investigate how this can be promoted and enhanced.

Chapter 9, Enhancing Students' Imagination and Intuition, reviews some of the excellent literature available on the subject of encouraging students to use their imaginations and intuitive processes. It makes sense that those who are interested in promoting the use of imagination and intuition with teachers would also be concerned with such encouragement for students. Obviously the ideas go hand in hand.

The final chapter of Pursuing the Elusive Image offers some Implications and Further Reflection. The primary function of this concluding chapter is to kindle further insights within the reader regarding teachers' everyday use of imagination and intuition.

This book may evoke more questions than it answers, but its intent is to spark interest in these topics rather than to be a definitive statement. Any look at such esoteric phenomena in teaching is highly individualized, and each reader is invited to ponder the themes and ideas as they may relate to your own teaching experience. It is my hope that as you read through the chapters you will visualize your own classroom situation as it has been or can be. I hope you ask yourself many of the questions to see if any of the insights presented here match your own. The art of teaching is not divulged through books, courses, or discussions. It is lived in the hearts and souls of inspired teachers who invest their talents in the true education of tomorrow's children.

CHAPTER 2

IMAGES
OF ARTISTIC TEACHERS

Imagination is more important than knowledge.

—Albert Einstein

In the first chapter I posed a few questions. Among them are: "Who is able 'to educate?' to enlighten?" and "What is so special about these good teachers who evoke such charged and excited responses from their students?" I contend that teachers who freely exercise their own imaginations and who utilize their intuitive capacities are more likely to engage their students in truly enjoyable and relevant learning. My image of a good teacher is that of a person who is continually engaging in imaginative ventures. Such a teacher imagines his/her classes even when not in the school, always picturing what has occurred and what will be happening in the classroom. These imaginative teachers can be listening to someone, watching a movie or otherwise involved and something will trigger a response that will cause them to imagine "How would that work in my classroom?" or "Wouldn't Susie Smith get a charge out of this?"

The ability to imagine is an essential ingredient to good teaching. One needs to be able to picture how an idea might be played out with a particular group of students in order to decide how to best present the idea in a lesson. Good lesson planning in general is a highly imaginative act. To me good lesson planning is picturing your students doing whatever it is you have planned for them and "seeing" how Johnny or Mary might respond in your mind's eye. You might decide to alter your approach as you picture yourself going through the lesson.

This ability to image is an essential part of any artistic endeavor. There is definitely an art to good teaching. Teachers who employ their imagination and intuition in the teaching process get excellent results with their students. Teachers who have been recognized for excellence are often termed "artistic" since they excel in the practice of their art (Eisner 1983).

Adept artists are intuitive as well as imaginative. The spontaneity and inventiveness displayed by good artists is also part of the repertoire of an exemplary teacher. The adjectives *imaginative* and *intuitive* are attributed to exemplary teaching throughout much of the educational literature. I have combed through writings which have similar ideas as mine. I summarize here some of the important similarities to aid in the imaging of "artistic teachers."

Louis J. Rubin (1985) defines "the artist teacher" in his book, *Artistry in Teaching.* He is not referring to a teacher of the fine arts per se, but rather he describes the general demeanor of an artistic teacher as one who is exceptional in terms of use of judgment and imagination. Rubin claims that such exceptional teachers "differ from ordinary teachers in that they function with consummate skill. Some, blessed with natural gifts, rely principally on instinct. Others, less intuitive, cultivate equally impressive artistry through practice and effort. In

so doing, they often borrow insight and confidence from
the methods of those whose talent is innate" (Rubin
1985, p. 15). He views these exceptional teachers as carrying out their daily activities "with unusual imagination and brilliance."

Rubin delineates three criteria for artistic teaching:
"(a) the choice of educational aims that have high worth,
(b) the use of imaginative and innovative ways to achieve
these aims, and (c) the pursuit of their achievement with
great skill and dexterity" (Rubin 1985, p. 16). He is quick
to point out that these three aspects must be framed in
the classroom to make sense for particular situations.
Good teachers are able to adapt to unexpected opportunities. He stresses the teacher's use of improvisation
and flexibility in order to create and recreate as situations dictate. There is a balance between organized planning and flowing with momentary serendipity in good
teachers. The "four primary attributes," which Rubin
(1985, p. 17) ascribes to highly artistic teachers, are:
"First, they made a great many teaching decisions intuitively; second, they had a strong grasp of their subject
as well as a perceptive understanding of their students;
third, they were secure in their competence and expected
to be successful; and fourth, they were exceedingly imaginative." Rubin's experiment with approximately three
hundred and fifty teachers took place rather informally
over the period of four years. He traveled about speaking
with different faculties and teachers at random during
the first couple of years. Then the random involvement
was systematized slightly as Rubin concentrated with
twenty selected schools. His main concern was self-
directed professional growth of teachers. Through faculty
meetings and telephone and mail communications to
faculty representatives, he made suggestions to teachers
for improvement and acted as a facilitator and "ener-
gizer" for teacher growth toward artistry. He relied on
communication with the teacher representatives to keep

informed of progress. Many of the characteristics of artistic teachers that Rubin describes were clarified through his observations in the schools and discussions with teachers.

Although he does not advocate formulae for good teaching, Rubin (1985, pp. 20-22) gives twelve practical suggestions for "teaching artistry" that help to define what it means to be an artistic teacher:

1. Focus on the subtleties of teaching—motivation, pacing, control—which invigorate basic instructional methods and subject matter.

2. Improvise tactics for reaching objectives and overcoming difficulties.

3. Take advantage of opportunities to clarify ideas and reinforce concepts.

4. Make use of intuition and hunch in modifying routine practices.

5. Set high expectations for yourself and your students.

6. Find the most efficient and expedient ways of getting things done.

7. Use temporary digressions on related topics to enrich lessons, stimulate interest, and increase pace.

8. Base your control of learning activities on student behavior.

9. Take pride in what you do and in the achievement of your students.

10. Concentrate on a few dominant goals, central to your purpose.

11. Respect your convictions.

12. Devote as much time as possible to whatever you enjoy most in teaching.

My own views are quite similar to those of Rubin's, particularly with regard to how exemplary or "artistic" teachers use their imagination and intuition. Rubin mentions that artistic teachers rely on their intuitive understanding of a situation and refers to this as "innate." He refers to "less intuitive" teachers as borrowing from those with inherent ability. I believe that everyone has intuitive capabilities, but as with any other competence, this often needs to be enhanced with practice and experience. It is much more difficult to analyze and discuss the ability to intuit than it is to examine what it means to use one's imagination. Indeed, as I supervised student teachers over the course of eight years at the University of Illinois, I clearly realized that some of my students appeared to be more intuitive than others. I could easily have dismissed this as some of them having been born to be teachers, but this use of intuition intrigued me. In weekly seminars I tried to find ways for those with the intuitive understanding to aid those less adept in this area. Sometimes I think I was simply trying to see if some of this ability would merely "rub off" on those who needed it. The process of "teaching teachers to teach" forced me to analyze not only my students' performances but also my own. Through this examination I became acutely aware of the value of the everyday use of intuition and imagination in the teaching process.

Another author, Elliot Eisner (1985a), also looks at teaching as an art form. Like Rubin and myself, Eisner sees the teacher as a true performer. Certainly a good teaching performance can be an aesthetic experience:

> There are classrooms in which what the teacher does—the way in which activities are orchestrated, questions asked, lectures given—constitutes a form of artistic expression. What occurs is a performance that provides intrinsic forms of satisfaction, so much so that

we use the adjectives and accolades usually applied to the formal arts to describe what the teacher does while teaching. (Eisner 1985a, p. 153)

What are these things that teachers do that make them comparable to artists? Eisner depicts artistic teachers as utilizing qualitative aspects of their intellects during classroom encounters. Teachers determine the quality of the environment for the students by designing the space, setting the mood, pacing the rhythm, and generally orchestrating the experience. Like a good jazz musician, a creative teacher needs to be "in tune" with the members of the class to quickly react to the emergent chords with a melodic or dissonant response. Eisner describes a teacher's use of innovation as artistic. Although he recognizes that even creative teachers need repertoires to draw upon, he feels that "prescription and routine do not dominate" the artistic teacher's daily activity (Eisner 1985a, p. 154). A good teacher knows how to utilize the routines in order to focus more attention on the class as developments occur. The teacher's creative energies are conserved for use at appropriate moments by not having to respond in a totally novel way every instant. "It is precisely the tension between automaticity and inventiveness that makes teaching, like any other art, so complex an undertaking" (Eisner 1985a, p. 154).

Eisner (1985a) further compares good teaching to art by pointing out that in good teaching the outcomes are ever emergent as an integral part of the process. Just as a painter does not know exactly what a final masterpiece will look like—one stroke leads to another; one hue, one shape inspires subsequent colors, tones, and forms—the creative teacher discovers with the students as activities pattern themselves through emerging interests and ideas. Certainly good teachers have goals in mind and often rather specific intentions are preconceived, just as a painter may have a mind's-eye image of what will appear on the canvas. But the art lies in the willingness to "go with the flow" and to create.

I am reminded of an experience that I had in a painting course in undergraduate school. Painting was never my medium, and I was struggling with a rather mundane still-life when the instructor came by and, pointing to a particular area of my canvas, he said "There, now you've got it! That's more like it!" I replied, "I just did that because it dripped." His words, "Well, let it drip! Let it drip!," have often echoed in my mind to inspire me in other creative endeavors—although painting is not among them.

What makes some teachers more willing to "let it drip" than others? Is spontaneity appropriate in classrooms? It seems that the thing one can always expect in a school is the unexpected. An artistic teacher can take an unplanned occurrence and make it "the teachable moment," whereas the craft-oriented teacher might look upon the same situation as an annoyance to tolerate.

Eisner (1983) compares good teachers to orchestra conductors creating a symphonic experience of harmonious activity in the classroom. He refers to the enormous satisfaction that one feels as a teacher when students become excited as they understand new ideas. The pride of accomplishment when students acknowledge that the teacher has positively affected their lives. "The aesthetic in teaching is the experience secured from being able to put your own signature on your own work—to look at it and say it was good" (Eisner 1983). As editor of the 1985 yearbook for the National Society for the Study of Education, Eisner (1985b) refers to the back-to-basics movement in American schools as reducing and limiting the scope of what is possible in educational settings. The contributors to the yearbook, *Learning and Teaching, The Ways of Knowing*, are collectively broadening the range of, not only what is acceptable for schooling, but what is necessary for education. Eisner uses the word "imagination" when describing good teaching but only alludes to the use of intuition through ideas such as responding to students' emerging needs and altering routines at appropriate times.

Rudolf Arnheim (1985) delves into the significance of the intuitive mode in learning. He reminds us that Descartes viewed intuition as more dependable than other methods of deduction. Arnheim cautions us to recognize that intuitive perception is as worthy as intellectual analysis. He is concerned that by not giving credence to the seriousness of intuition in all areas of knowledge acquisition, we may be crippling the minds of students. Although his message is directed toward the learner, or how one acquires knowledge, the point can be made that a good teacher who is cognizant of the "double-edged mind" of the learner will certainly understand the necessity for the intuitive mode in the teaching process. Many aspects of the teaching/learning process are reciprocal. As Dewey (1910) has pointed out to us, one cannot have taught unless someone has learned.

It is my belief at this time that the use of one's imagination and the use of one's intuition overlap to a great extent. However, I feel that it is the imagination that one uses to plan curriculum for the classroom and it is the intuition that one uses to implement the curriculum. William Schubert (1975) studied teacher's use of imagination in curriculum planning. He developed the term IMPRO or "Imaginative projection" which refers to a teacher's ability to imagine certain aspects of the curriculum as these elements will be implemented.

> *General propositions do not decide concrete cases. The decision will depend on a judgment or intuition more subtle than any articulate major premise.*
>
> —Oliver Wendell Holmes, Jr., in Lochner v. New York, 198 U.S. (1905)

Schubert's method (1975) of utilizing the imagination in planning was initially meant to help teachers with situation-specific problems regarding the implementation of pre-defined curricula which did not fit a particular classroom situation. Without mentioning the word "intuition" Schubert refers to spontaneous decision-making processes and judgments that need "to quickly coalesce, be acted upon, and moved past" (Schubert 1975, p. 179). The IMPRO method calls for teachers to imagine the possibilities and their probable consequences related to curriculum implementation.

This manner of planning has wide applications. I think that it is representational of how teachers do, in fact, plan. "Planning" is not limited to the writing of lesson plans. On the contrary, often the writing can get in the way as a teacher conjures up the image of the class and how they, as a whole, and as individuals in the class will react to certain ideas and activities. Such imagining can be done alone, in the car, or in the bath. One can also utilize a colleague or other willing person to help conjure up images of possibilities and their consequences.

Dewey (1916) leads us to imagine teachers who are democratic in their approach to the classroom. Dewey's conception of the democratic teacher is akin to that of the artistic teacher in a few respects. A democratic teacher not only allows for, but encourages student participation in all aspects of classroom life. Dewey (1916) argued that we must move from the "psychological" to the "logical." By this he meant that we should structure learning experiences that begin with the student's interests. A Deweyan teacher needs to ascertain the deep rooted interests of each student and allow for individualization in the pursuit of that which makes learning meaningful for them. It is through these experiences which interest the learners that they will gradually become acquainted with the "disciplines of knowledge."

The teacher is instrumental in guiding them toward these disciplines. Thus, a Deweyan teacher is truly "educating" or leading out. Although Dewey is mainly concerned with the democratic idea of classroom life, his descriptions of teachers are similar to those of highly imaginative and intuitive professionals.

Joseph Schwab (1969, 1970, 1971, 1973) emphasizes a practical inquiry for curriculum research. He looks to practicing teachers for analysis of the teaching process. Schwab brings to mind the image of the good teacher as a curriculum developer and practical researcher. Schwab (1971) has delineated three "arts of eclectic." A good teacher-as-curriculum-developer would possess the capacity to, first, mate theoretical or disciplinary knowledge and perspectives with the needs and interests of the learners; second, adapt theoretical or disciplinary knowledge and perspectives to the needs and interests of the learners; and finally, produce a selection of courses of action and foresee the possible consequences of these actions.

It is obvious that Schwab's image of a good teacher-as-curriculum-developer is that of a well-rounded individual with varied experiences. The teacher would need to be well-read in literature, philosophy, psychology, etc., as well as educational theory. Armed with this repertoire of theory and practice, the artistic teacher would interpret classroom situations as they arise. Obviously such teachers would be creating their own practical theories regarding life in classrooms by an eclectic selection of knowledge from existing theories with the situational applications they make on a daily basis. Schubert (1986, p. 299) provides us with the image of such Schwabian teachers as operating "on a body of precedent of past experience that helps them to respond to practical problems, derive meaning, generate imaginative alternative possibilities for action, and judge the moral and educative value of consequences of curriculum that they create with students." To me this is describing teachers' use of intuition as well as their imaginations.

> *Too much sanity may be madness and the maddest of all, to see life as it is and not as it should be.*
>
> —Man of La Mancha

Maxine Greene (1981) views the aesthetic imagination as that which enables us to see things as they could be otherwise. Greene is a proponent of the power of aesthetic awareness in education. In earlier writings, Greene (1973) provides us with the image of the teacher as an isolate, alienated by the nature of the profession. The teacher is alone in a group of younger individuals. Artistic teachers may begin to question their own images of good teaching. Without supportive colleagues, teachers may question their decisions in daily classroom situations. In a subsequent work, Greene (1978) conjures up the image of a good teacher as a gifted gardener, carefully seeding, watering, fertilizing, weeding and pruning the "landscapes of learning." A well-cultivated classroom sprouts imagination and creativity. Greene's image of a good teacher is one who is self-empowered with a "wide-awakeness" (1978). This form of consciousness in a classroom setting depicts a good teacher as ever alert and attentive to the details within the complexity of the environment. A "wide-awake" teacher is one who is sincerely fascinated with life and demonstrates this interest with the students.

Greene states that good teachers are "those who can create the kinds of conditions that move diverse young persons to take their own initiatives and move beyond what is taught" (Greene 1978, p. 83). Greene sees good teachers as those who have a variety of perspectives through which they view the world:

They need to be the kinds of teachers equipped to make practical judgments on the grounds of what they have learned in the realms of theory, what they have discovered from empirical research, what they understand about children and youth, and what they understand about themselves. They need to be the kinds of teachers who can make their own thinking visible to the young, to manifest the ways in which the modes of procedure in each domain are put to work, to submit their own judgments to the critical scrutiny of those they teach, to open perspectives, to open worlds. (Greene 1978, p. 83)

It is important to continually analyze what makes an outstanding teacher unique. Through this process we progress in our understanding of good teaching and gain valuable insight into ways we might improve our own and other's performance. Through examination of these various images of artistic teachers new perspectives and understandings are gleaned to enhance the overall perception of the remarkably complex teaching process.

PART II

EXPRESSIONS OF IMAGINATION AND INTUITION

*And as imagination bodies forth
The forms of things unknown, the poet's pen
Turns them to shapes, and gives to
    airy nothing
A local habitation and a name.*

—Shakespeare in
A Midsummer Night's Dream

What do we mean by the terms *imagination* and *intuition?* By looking into the origins and past definitions of words we can rejuvenate some of the "past power" of these words (van Manen 1984). One of the goals of this book is to attach meaning to these terms as they apply to teaching. Therefore, the terms are also examined as they are defined by teachers. These complex terms do not have succinct definitions. As we ponder various meanings and the scope of usage in classrooms, further insights develop regarding imagination and intuition. The disparate definitions discussed here are not meant to confuse the reader, but rather to provoke enough consideration of the terms in all their complexity.

How would you define these terms? What does imagination mean to you? Are there special connotations which come to mind when you consider how teachers use their imaginations as they plan learning experiences and facilitate these events in the classroom? What does intuition mean to you? When and how might a teacher use her intuition in the classroom setting? Is it appropriate to rely on intuitive insights when making judgments regarding student learning?

CHAPTER 3

DEFINITION
OF TERMS

What is Imagination?

The word imagination is routinely used in various contexts. As with many such overworked terms, the word has taken on divergent meanings. Gilbert Ryle, in *The Concept of Mind* (1949), tells us that the word imagination refers to an extensive array of activities including: pretending, acting, impersonating, fancying and imaging. Sutherland (1971, p. 1) cautions that imagination "is in fact one of those useful but misleading words which can fit without any perceptible jarring into a good many contexts." *Webster's Ninth New Collegiate Dictionary* (1987, p. 600) defines imagination as "the act or power of forming a mental image of something not present to the senses or never before wholly perceived in reality; creative ability; ability to confront and deal with a problem: resourcefulness; the thinking or active mind: interest; a creation of the mind, especially: an idealized or poetic creation; fanciful or empty assumption."

Etymologically, the word "imagination" is derived from the Latin word *imago*, which means an image or representation. Usually when using the verb *to imagine* we are alluding to this root meaning of invoking an image—visualizing. Correspondingly the noun *imagination* often denotes conception or visualization of something. However through continual usage the noun *imagination* and the adjective *imaginative* have evolved to connote much more than mere representation. Robin Barrow (1988, p. 81) has examined some of the vernacular uses of the word imaginative: "Some people appear to use the word as a synonym for 'sensitive,' others for 'creative,' 'inventive,' 'reflective,' and so on."

Jean Paul Sartre, in *The Psychology of Imagination* (1948), defines imagination as being intentional, conscious, and apart from reality. Harold Rugg, in *Imagination* (1963, p. 36), states that "Imagination is the instrument of discovery . . . discovery *is* imagined conception." Rugg echoes Immanuel Kant (1781, 1787) when he makes a distinction between productive or creative imagination and reproductive imagination. Creative imagination includes memory and is based in perception. Rugg says that the primary distinction between man and animals is the ability to solve problems symbolically, in one's imagination. Samuel Coleridge (1817) also made use of Kant's productive imagination in relating his own differentiation between primary and secondary imagination. Primary imagination is analogous to Kant's productive imagination. Coleridge sees the secondary imagination as that which operates in the creative arts. It is the process that idealizes and consolidates disparate images and ideas. By diffusing and dissipating some of the image fragments and qualities, the secondary imagination is able to create and re-create and put life to thoughts.

T. P. Hohler (1982) reviews Fichte's *Grundlage* of 1794 in *Imagination and Reflection: Intersubjectivity.* Hohler declares that imagination is an act of the reflective consciousness. The reflective subject abstracts from self-awareness. This retrieval is the preliminary step toward imagination. In the imaginative process there is an intentionality of the subject. Imagination is a deduction of representation. He refers to an "intuiting activity of the imagination" (Hohler 1982, p. 74). He claims that the imagination is the product of, or produces this intuiting activity. Fichte, himself, said that "Only for the imagination is there such a thing as time" (Hohler 1982, p. 25). One teacher referred to "the fullness of time" as she explained what imagination is to her: "The imagination is what enables us to connect. Without connection we don't know anything. Without the imagination there are no wholes. In imaginative fullness there is a context for a fact."

Barell (1980, p. 3) declares that "playing with ideas" is at the heart of the creative process "it reflects the basic relationship between science and imagination, and more importantly, between imagination and all human ways of knowing and doing." He states that playful imaginative activity is what Einstein was doing at age sixteen when he visualized himself riding along a ray of light to study its properties. Some teachers have referred to the idea of being able to visualize something when defining imagination: "It is something that you can see but nobody else can."

Jacob Bronowski, in *The Identity of Man* (1971, p. 58), claims that the "invention of these ideas and their interplay in language is imagination—the making of images inside our heads. In this sense science is as much a play of the imagination as poetry is." Do you visualize when you imagine? How does that help you in teaching?

I remember times when I would envision my class in my mind's eye. The images were not still, it was similar to viewing a video tape with continually changing motion. Usually I would see the class from my own viewpoint, through my own eyes. But sometimes I would visualize myself in the scene, looking in from a "God's eye view" at what was going on. Sometimes I was in the process of planning a new lesson as I was visualizing my class and how they might respond, but often I was replaying the day's events in my mind's eye. This recap would aide in my evaluation of the day's events and lead toward planning activities for tomorrow. It was never a forced process, it seemed like a natural way to survey the day. It appeared to be a normal occurrence.

This daydreaming, or picturing your classroom in your mind, allows you to explore possibilities—endless possibilities. As one teacher put it: "Imagination is thinking of the various possibilities of a certain situation." To her it was important to realize what could or could not be accomplished: ". . . the things that are possible and the things that aren't possible and the things that you would like to be possible, given a certain situation." She referred to making an invention: "You have to know scientifically what will work—you also have to go after what has never been done before, you don't even know if it could work, so it's not in the realm of reality—you don't know if it's possible."

Karen Hansen (1988, p. 138) also defines imagination in terms of possibilities: "Imagination is what allows us to envision possibilities in or beyond the actualities in which we are immersed." The imagination is capable of eliminating boundaries or conventional limitations to our thinking. Schubert (1975, p. 4) describes Imaginative Projection (IMPRO) as:

> A curriculum decision-making strategy that enables curriculum planners and implementers to generate possibilities, project probable consequences, formulate and entertain hypotheses in action, and assess the consonance of hypotheses with aims and principles. It refers to a process of inventing solutions to problematic curriculum situations, a process which is simultaneously based upon defensible ethical principles. It is a situation analysis.

While the imagination has the capacity to disregard restrictions, often when particular limits are set the imagination grows within the boundaries. This may at first appear to be an incongruous statement, however an artist would recognize this as fact. The sculptor chooses among various media and as she selects a particular clay or stone she is setting limits. As she decides the size and scope of the sculpture she further restricts herself. Within these predetermined boundaries the imagination takes shape. The performance artist decides on a particular subject and setting. He creates the performance from these confines. You do not have to be an accomplished artist to have experienced this phenomenon. Have you ever looked in the refrigerator to make dinner only to find a limited amount of possible ingredients? It is often the limitations which cause us to become creative.

Many teachers envision situations this way by considering the possibilities and recognizing the constraints under which they are placed. Some typical classroom restrictions include space, time and materials. As I interact with teachers regarding the use of their own imaginations, many have become more cognizant of the visualization that takes place. One teacher mentioned to me: "since we've met I'm more conscious about it. I actually picture more images in my mind than I used to and I think that's helpful. I image when making the plans and then when evaluating them afterwards." This same teacher reminds us that the imagination is a highly individualized commodity. Not everyone uses visual imagery. She is more comfortable with other avenues of the imagination: "I usually have a dialogue with myself. I have a conversation about the possibilities of what could happen." Do you tend to visualize when you imagine or do you use other forms, such as hearing as the main mode to conjure up an event or experience?

What does it mean to look at all the possibilities when imagining? Sometimes it means wanting to get an idea across to a group of students and conjuring various ways to present the concept. Repetition is often a necessity in classrooms. To alleviate boredom, teachers constantly dream up diverse manners of presentation and practice. One teacher called this "active imagination": "When I actively imagine I take the same concept and try to think of it, exhaust it with as many situations as possible."

To many teachers imagination in teaching implies creativity. One teacher had a hard time calling herself "imaginative" because she does not regard herself as an artistic person. She does consider teaching an art, however, and certainly considers herself to be a good teacher. So as our discussions proceeded, she discovered that indeed she could describe her teaching as imaginative. Are you an imaginative teacher? Do you want to be? Do you think good teachers are imaginative?

Being able to think creatively is perceived as being imaginative. The words imaginative and creative are often used interchangeably. When defining imagination one teacher said "Imaginative teaching would imply instruction that is creative. Imagination and creativity probably are very close." When I asked what she meant as creativity she responded: "Probably conjuring up something that is either new to you or new to you and others. Whatever it may be. Whether it's music or technique or a drawing. A sentence." This idea of originality or discovery is an integral part of Rugg's (1963) definition of imagination. Barrow (1988, p. 84) suggests that to be innovative or to envisage the "unusual" is fundamental to the imagination:

> The criteria of imagination are, I suggest, unusualness and effectiveness. To be imaginative is to have the inclination and ability consciously to conceive of the unusual and effective in particular contexts.

I believe there is a strong link between imagination and intelligence although, admittedly, there are many highly "intelligent" people who are not extremely imaginative. Creative thinkers throughout the ages have been thought of as intelligent. For example, Einstein used imaging to formulate his theory of relativity. He views imagination as being "more important than knowledge." I think the imagination assists with attainment of knowledge. The uniqueness of thought of highly intelligent individuals is an aspect of being imaginative. Barrow (1988, p. 89) has a similar view of an imaginative person. She uses the word educated rather than intelligent: "I would argue that an educated person, as distinct from a well-trained person or an indoctrinated person, must necessarily possess imagination."

The notion of love came up with different teachers when defining imagination: "love of subject matter is an important factor in being imaginative in teaching that subject." "Imagination is letting your love be translated into your classroom." Teachers talked about loving teaching, loving their students and showing "passion" for what they are teaching when defining imagination in the classroom: "I see imagination as being a passionate activity, because it is a loving thing to do."

To one teacher imagination is "pure and simply completely crucial. There is no education without it. Period." There is a feeling that the imagination renders us capable of putting knowledge into context: "The imagination is what enables us to connect and without connection we don't know anything. Without the imagination, there is no such thing as a whole, there are only a whole bunch of disassociated parts, which are completely without meaning." The teacher's use of imagination makes things "come alive" for students. Coleridge's (1817) idea of the "secondary imagination" amalgamates diverse images and ideas, thereby creating and recreating and giving life to thoughts.

Kieran Egan and Dan Nadaner (1988) consider the use of the imagination essential to teaching and learning:

imagination . . . is the heart of any truly educational experience; it is not something split off from "the basics' or disciplined thought or rational inquiry, but is the quality that can give them life and meaning; it is not something belonging properly to the arts, but is central to all areas of the curriculum; it is not something to ornament our recreational hours, but is the hard pragmatic center of all effective human thinking . . . Stimulating the imagination is not an alternative educational activity to be argued for in competition with other claims; it is a prerequisite to making any activity educational. (Egan and Nadaner 1988, p. ix)

Do you agree that the use of your imagination is crucial to good teaching? How does a teacher's use of her imagination kindle students' imaginations? Is it the responsibility of the teacher to engage the students' imaginations at all times?

What is Intuition?

An understanding of the term *intuition* is often abstruse and vague. In the vernacular, intuitions are often referred to as "hunches," "instincts," "gut feelings" or "guesses." As a form of action, to intuit is replaced by verbs as "to see", "to know," "to sense," "to perceive" or "to feel." Often these words are preceded by the word "just." "I just knew," "it just felt right," "I just sensed that." Thus, meaning, "it is nothing more than that" or "I cannot explain it any further." The sensations or feelings related to intuition are often sensed within one's body. Consequently, we have expressions such as "I feel it in my bones," "I know it in my heart" or "it was a gut reaction." The concept of intuition appears incomprehensible through calculated logical inquiry, and therefore difficult to concisely define in words. Intuition is something you instinctively feel inside yourself. As such it challenges rational explanation.

Etymologically, *intuition* is derived from the Latin verb *intueri*, which means "to look upon." Therefore the idea of looking or seeing is intrinsic in the origins of the word. *Webster's Ninth New Collegiate Dictionary* (1987, p. 635) defines intuition as "immediate apprehension or cognition; knowledge or conviction gained by intuition; the power or faculty of attaining to direct knowledge or cognition without evident rational thought and inference; quick and ready insight." Immediacy or spontaneity is a fundamental element of any definition of intuition. When you intuit there is an apprehension of knowledge without going through the steps of logic. A perceptible power within when you "just know it's right."

In their book *Awakening the Inner Eye: Intuition in Education*, Nel Noddings and Paul Shore (1984, p. 57) define intuition as follows: "Intuition is that function that connects objects directly in phenomena. This direct contact yields something we might call 'knowledge.'" Noddings and Shore view intuition as a feat which involves the use of the will in which the logical processes are accelerated. They see this occurring in the conscious mind, unlike others who espouse intuition as an unconscious process. Some authors have used the term intuition to connote an instinctive comprehension or realization which is not invoked through the conscious mind.

Carl Jung, in *Psychological Types* (1923), alleges that intuition stems from the unconscious. Eric Berne, in *Intuition and Ego States: The Origins of Transactional Analysis* (1977), tells us that intuition is a perception that first occurs in the unconscious and is then brought out into a conscious state.

Many teachers had great difficulty with the definition of intuition. Some felt that what I was calling intuition was actually what might be termed "perceptiveness." Certainly intuition is a kind of perception. Greene opposes intuition to the intellect and says that intuition is a particular property of perception. Greene (1978, p. 216) demonstrates the importance she places on this mode of knowing by stating "perceptual reality ought always to be considered one of the multiple realities available to us: a recognizable set of experiences, once they are reflected upon, characterized by a distinctive mode of attention, one too many people have repressed or refused." Arnheim (1985) states that intuition is one specific property of perception, namely, its ability to apprehend directly the effect of interaction taking place in a gestalt situation. Intuition is a part of every cognitive act. The intellect as well operates at all levels of cognition. There is definitely a link between the intellect and intuition.

Jerome Bruner, in *The Process of Education* (1978), claims that intuition refers to good guesses. As applied to problem-solving, Bruner views intuition as an implicit perception of the total process. Max Wertheimer, in *Productive Thinking* (1945), refers to the problem-solving aspects of intuition also. He argues that total immersion in a problem leads to the intuitive leaps of discovery. After comprehensive interviews with Einstein, Wertheimer portrays him as a visual thinker using feelings and imagination to guide him rather than a rational approach to important insights. The analysis occurs in retrospect.

René Descartes, in *Rules for the Directions of the Mind* (Blom, trans. 1977), tells us: "By intuition I understand not the fluctuating testimony of the senses nor the misleading judgment that proceeds from the blundering constructions of imagination but the conception which an unclouded and attentive mind gives us so readily and distinctly that we are wholly freed from doubt about what we understand." Although he stresses the reliability of intuitions, Descartes is somewhat negating the validity of the imagination.

My own definition is that "intuition is a grasp at knowledge that connects the subconscious and the conscious mind—pulling prior knowledge synthesized in the subconscious to the conscious level at an opportune moment for immediate insight" (Jagla 1992, p. 66).

A few of the teachers came up with succinct definitions for intuition: "Intuition is the name I'd apply to an action or reaction that is felt or sensed, often not resulting from any identifiable thought process." Another defines intuition by saying that: "It's listening to the song in the heart rather than the song in the head. Following the gut, allowing the gut to lead you sometimes." Besides "just going with the hunch," he perceives intuition in a more deliberate approach: "With intuition, I tend to be a little more scientific about it than many people. I think that it really is built on observable factors, but we can't always verbalize what they were. What was it that you saw that told you to do that? Now where are we going to go with this? How far are we going to get with it? Sometimes the intuition comes in with answering the question for yourself. Is this class going to go better if I tell it where to go or if the students tell it where to go?"

As with other aspects of both imagination and intuition, some teachers I spoke with expressed their definitions of intuition differently as they reflected further regarding these complex issues. During an initial interview, one teacher said: "When I first received your questionnaire my definition of intuition was just sort of going on gut level—doing things without thinking about them first. Since we've talked today I've decided it isn't just acting spontaneously. It's thinking on the spot *and* reacting to those thoughts by acting accordingly."

Another teacher refined his definition of intuition through reflection and conversation. During an initial interview he referred to intuition in terms of perception for the purpose of decision-making: "I think intuition is picking up what the kids are saying to you in their non-verbal ways or interpreting even their verbal cues. That's your intuition. It's really being able to perceive where they're coming from. Where is their energy? I need to be able to read them, know where they're coming from and make a selection of an activity that would be useful at that time. The editing that takes place, the split-second decisions, the intuition gives me the knowledge. You're a fool if you drive off without finding out where they're going first." This corresponds with the way Rubin (1985, p. 61) describes the teacher's use of intuition in the classroom: "the teacher makes a rapid assessment, assimilates the available cues, and forms a conclusion."

During a subsequent conversation, the teacher placed more emphasis on the idea of judgment when defining intuition. Like other teachers he spoke of becoming more adept at the intuitive judgment process as his experience grew: "I would say that intuition is a process where one would make a multi-sensory obser-vation and formulate some type of a judgment. I think that you store certain situations in your memory bank and it's a matter of retrieving them. My judgment process was slower in my first years of teaching because I didn't have anything in my memory bank. But after you deal with kids or personalities for X amount of time, you become more apt in judging and being able to pick up what's going on, then your decision-making, your judg-ment is much quicker." The notion of improvement in speed and accuracy regarding discretionary decisions being aided by one's storehouse of memories is reminis-cent of Schwab's (1971) repertoire as he describes his "Arts of Eclectic."

Teachers correlated intuition with assurance as they defined it: "It's the feeling of confidence to go with some-thing that just occurs to you spontaneously." Many teachers believe that these intuitive "feelings" are con-nected to confidence. Through experience one gains con-fidence. Similarly as teachers gain experience in the classroom their intuitive capacities also expand. Some teachers were hesitant to give precise definitions for intuition. One teacher spoke of spontaneously knowing what is the right thing to do in the classroom at a given moment when something planned is not working: "I don't know if it's intuition. Maybe it's just confidence . . . To me it just seems obvious. Now, is that intuition? I don't know."

Are you an intuitive teacher? Is it necessary for a teacher to use intuition to be a good teacher?

Is there a Bond between Imagination and Intuition?

> Imaginative play is a key that opens the door of intuition, and its practical value is readily visible.
>
> —Frances E. Vaughan (1979, p. 153)

I have chosen to discuss imagination and intuition together. I perceive the two ideas hand in hand. Other teachers related the issues when defining the terms: "Intuition is what we use that enables us to trust what our imagination dishes up for us. Intuition is the enabler. Imagination is what is enabled." When referring to the teacher's role in educating as leading one from darkness into light, one teacher said that it was "intuition as well as imagination that guides you through the darkness . . . It is hard often to distinguish between intuition and imagination. Imagination deals in more concrete terms. One can have intuitions that thus and so will occur. But the actual occurrence comes about through the imagination."

I have often felt that as teachers we use our imaginations more in planning and evaluating and our intuitions during implementation of lessons and direct contact with students. Some teachers agreed with this. One teacher felt that we use our imaginations to prepare us for intuitive insights: "I think if you imagined all kinds of possibilities beforehand, then you're open to go with one that comes up at the moment. So imagination has prepared you to feel free to act intuitively."

Another teacher believes intuition triggers the imagination. She does not feel that imagination is necessarily a premeditated, cognitive reaction: "Imagination in teaching is often the response caused by intuition. Imagination is not, however, a cognitive process planned to be an awakening fantasy. There are things that set off the imagination that sometimes you are not aware of." I believe that the use of the imagination is indeed cognitive and much of the time it is a deliberate and conscious act. When planning presentations one might consciously develop a learning experience to evoke particular responses from students. You might intuitively know what you would like to accomplish, then your imagination can take over to embellish the plan.

One teacher regards imagination and intuition as interrelated and essential elements of any teaching day: "Intuition is part of my diagnosis . . . Imagination builds my fund of knowledge and activities of what I can do for my objective of the day. I've got to put the two together to come up with my day."

Another teacher sees a correlation between imagination and intuition with regard to lesson planning: "I use intuition in lesson planning quite a bit. It ties in closely with your imagination. Will this work? With this class, yes. With this class, maybe not." He mentioned one time when he had spent a lot of time preparing a lesson, but just as he walked into the classroom he realized that it was not going to work. Whether you label it intuition or not, many teachers have had this same experience. Something internal just lets you know when to change your plans and when to follow through.

One teacher spoke about reacting intuitively to a particular student's imagination: "Every once in a while a student will come up with an idea, or a way of looking at something that hadn't occurred to me." He related an account of a girl in a remedial English class who asked the question, regarding the story "The Wizard of Oz": "What if it wasn't a dream? What if Dorothy really went to Oz?" These questions intrigued the teacher to investigate further and he discovered what author Lyman Frank Baum had in mind: "One day's worth of research convinced me that he believed she went to Oz. The movie doesn't depict that, but the book does. That she actually went there, and went back several times, and that she was eventually able to go back and forth quite often." His intuition guided him to investigate the girl's imaginings. This in turn directed him to a subsequent use of his own imagination in planning a lesson for an oral communications class, based on this episode. He used the girl's initial questions, "What if it wasn't a dream? What if Dorothy really went to Oz?", as story starters for his class. The students came up with some highly imaginative tales.

To me it makes sense to discuss teachers' use of imagination and their use of intuition together. Are good teachers necessarily both imaginative **and** intuitive? Are these qualities you would apply to your own teaching?

CHAPTER 4

FURTHER UNDERSTANDING IN CONTEXT

The upcoming examples of teachers using their imagination and intuition in teaching are meant to help clarify the meanings attached to these complex terms. Reference was made to classroom settings in much of the definition chapter. This chapter departs from mere definition of terms and delves into how imagination and intuition manifest themselves into everyday classroom usage.

The discussion of examples of use of teachers' imaginations is separated into two sections. The first of these sections addresses how teachers' use their imaginations while faced with a group of students in the classroom. The second section is concerned with the role of the teacher's imagination while planning lessons. While some may view these as arbitrary distinctions, since planning and implementation are so closely related, I think it is worthwhile to consider the ideas independently.

The section on teachers' use of intuition is less lengthy. This in no way reflects the notion that imagination is more important in the lives of teachers. It does point out the difficulty experienced when verbalizing ideas regarding intuition. I believe that one's intuition comes into play continually during the course of a regular teaching day, quite often unnoticed.

Teachers' Use of Imagination
within the Classroom Setting

A friend gave an example of her college age daughter, who has had a difficult time understanding chemistry. She is presently in a class with an "imaginative" teacher, who has provided some enlightenment: "She's had to learn all these isolated things and she's never seen how they went together or had any reason to see, she's always had to just learn them isolated. So here's somebody, who, for the first time, has given her a context. All of a sudden it's all making marvelous sense. Without the imagination there are no wholes, there are only disassociated parts." Imaginative teachers tend to put themselves in the place of the students, providing the necessary background and framework for ideas to make sense. Not only do we need to provide a relevant context for our students, it is necessary to have legitimate interest in and enthusiasm for the subjects being taught and for the group of students with whom we are working to foster understanding.

A college music teacher coined the phrase "the fullness of time" and the idea of "fullness" in general, which refers to the context. She recounted in detail a lecture she gave in music history on Correlli, who is a composer she did not care for. She knew the subject matter inside and out. She knew the facts of Correlli's life, where he studied, what he did, what he wrote when, why he wrote it and where he was going next. In other words she was well-planned to be able to impart every factual detail of the composer's life to the students. However, she feels the information was not enough: "I didn't have any sense of mystery of the man whatsoever. I just knew all this stuff. So what I lacked then was any sense of imaginative fullness of Correlli and history. Part of the imagination is a sense of things always in context—the passing of time. Correlli, not just as Correlli, but reaching backwards and reaching forwards and being part of a thread of history." An unimaginative presentation in any classroom setting is typically one lacking in context or "fullness." The dry presentation of facts is not usually the best way to get information across for relevant understanding.

The current back-to-basics need for efficiency is unfortunately often responsible for factual presentations that may be lacking in imaginative demonstration. A sad commentary regarding our profession right now is that often teachers are made to feel that the maximum must be covered in the minimum of time. There seems to be little opportunity to allow for the "fullness of time." I see movement in the direction of providing background knowledge for students, tapping what they already know about a subject in order to make new information more relevant. Being "connected" seems to have a lot to do with the use of the imagination. Imaginative teachers know how to make these connections in order to make things come alive for students in meaningful contexts.

The idea of confidence was already mentioned in reference to definitions of intuition. The music teacher spoke of fear versus confidence and what happens when a teacher is not "connected" or lacking in imagination: "When I feel that cut off from the connectedness to the fullness of things, I feel very frightened inside. I feel lost, I feel isolated . . . and I don't know how to proceed. When I get into that shape, anything that I do is governed by fear, rather than by confidence . . . I think of that Correlli lecture and I think of how profoundly empty it was . . . I had to run faster and faster to avoid seeing that." Beginning teachers are often fearful. Afraid of losing control of the class, afraid the students will not like them and sometimes afraid to be imaginative. I teach methods classes to preservice teachers. Students delight in listening to ideas for imaginative lessons, how others have imaginatively arranged their time and materials to present meaningful lessons. Invariably, the majority of these soon-to-be-teachers conclude for themselves that they will "try that" in some distant year after they have "taught for awhile." Fear or lack of confidence often holds teachers back from being creative and using their imaginations to the fullest in the classroom.

In contrast to the emptiness of the non-imaginative Correlli lecture, the music teacher previously mentioned cited an example of a class in which Mozart was the subject. Since she enjoys Mozart so much she was able to transmit some of that excitement. An important aspect brought out through this story is the need for interaction with the individuals in a class: "I really led the class into who Mozart was, because I love Mozart so much. Everything that I'm saying was new and Mozart was just alive in the room in my mind. Because he was alive in my mind . . . and he was alive in the minds of those who were with me." Enthusiasm and excitement for the subject matter can spark the imagination and carry a lesson in such a manner as to enliven all involved. Involvement is also a key issue. When a teacher is imaginative she is absorbed in the lesson. Often this genuine excitement is enough to ignite the imaginations of the students. Sometimes just "hooking" one student is enough to keep things alive and let the involvement spread. Interacting with the class can help make ideas come alive: ". . . as a teacher I've always depended on . . . whoever it was in the class who I could count on for an interaction, because they become part of my own imaginative process . . . bringing Mozart alive for Richard was part of bringing Mozart alive for myself . . . and back and forth. So without Richard, I couldn't have brought Mozart to life."

One teacher referred to good teaching as carrying on a conversation with thirty at one time. The trick is to relate and interact with all students. It is this engagement that enlivens the classroom. It takes an imaginative person to truly engage all the students in a class at any given time. There are some students who would rather not be bothered and do not wish to put forth the effort to use their own imaginations, they would rather have a dry factual rendering of the material at hand. Usually these are older students who have been taught in this manner for most of their lives. The use of the imagination can bring us such joy, but it can be fearful to those who view it as uncharted territory. Imaginative and confident teachers are able to instill this confidence and imagination in their pupils.

An important part of being an imaginative and interactive teacher is to allow yourself some vulnerability. This is often where the fear sets in and teachers back off from trying imaginative approaches. It is important to leave yourself open to interactions with students. Traditionally the teacher has her place, the students have theirs. The teacher is the "guardian of the facts." These facts are then imparted to the students, a test or other assessment is administered by the teacher, after "mastery" we move on to the next set of facts. No one is really threatened in such a situation, all feel safe in their roles. Yet really opening up to the imaginative interaction strips away some boundaries for all. It can be exciting, fun and meaningful but without confidence of self a teacher may be wary to explore all the possibilities. Management problems keep some teachers from allowing for more creativity, i.e., the messiness involved with painting, the amount of time and energy involved to mark creative stories: "It takes a lot of energy to do that. They're not going to do it unless they feel really confident . . . In that way I think that teachers stifle kids."

One important way that teachers use their imaginations in the classroom is by becoming a part of the learning process with the students: "If the teacher isn't experiencing in that moment whatever it is and discovering it in that moment, whatever it is, then no learning is going to occur." A teacher told a story of a bright little boy in the first grade in an inner city classroom. They had been writing. She would have the children scribble on paper since they could not yet form many letters. Students would then "read" their stories: "Michael drew this wonderful continuous random line all over the page going in and out and all over the place, with incredible concentration for a young child. He couldn't wait to read it and he came up. He read it, he turned his head to go with it . . . It went all the way to completion and it stopped. I want very much to know what Michael was doing, but I know that whatever learning to read is and what learning to write is—he was beginning to do both." Here is a teacher who trusted her imagination and allowed for appropriate interaction and her own vulnerability. Because of this she was able to motivate a student to completely "write" and "read" a story even though he did not yet know how to form letters. She is allowing the student's experience to teach herself and other students.

Within the same classroom setting, there was a girl named Twana. She had difficulty with the writing process. One day she had written all the letters, A through Z and then she wrote numbers, 1 through 7. She was eager to read, so she came up. She was so excited and overwhelmed by reading what she had written aloud to the class that she opened her mouth and just about nothing came out at all. The teacher had been having the students read to each other in little groups before they came up to read to the class. Twana had been in a group with Michael and another boy. After she tried a couple of times and nothing was happening, the teacher asked if she would like the two boys to come up and help her read. She nodded her head. Michael looked at her paper and said "This is the letters story." Then they all read the letters. Then he said "And this is the numbers story." Then they all read the numbers. Twana went back to her seat radiant—she had written two stories. The teacher was quite moved by Michael's insight: "The wisdom of that little boy—that's what I'm after—an absolutely optimum. I don't get it at that level too often, he's an extraordinary child—God, I love that child. That is the extreme of what I'm after. That child was in possession of his own soul and nobody could take that away from him. He knew the value of what he was giving." Did the teacher lose control of the class because she allowed a six year-old boy to come up with a solution she couldn't find? I think rather her confidence allowed for this most meaningful interaction to happen. She had enough confidence in herself to learn from and with the children.

Another teacher gave some examples of the use of her imagination in the classroom which have to do with experiencing along with the students: "I think that it is very important to wonder out loud in front of the children. Sometimes, what I do is I pretend I'm in fourth grade. 'I have this problem now, I just divided it, what do I do next?' . . . But sometimes, in wondering out loud, I'll ask them a question and I'll try to make them see I'm asking that question because I don't know the answer. So they can see that adults go through that wondering process also." Wondering out loud is a terrific technique at all age levels. It takes some imagination on the part of the teacher to think like the students and "wonder" as the students themselves would. Some students will just naturally do this and are reinforced by the process, other students benefit from the example of being shown how to ponder and speculate about ideas.

Most imaginative teachers are not afraid to get involved and have fun with the students. In a U. S. History class, a high school teacher was taking his classes through a unit which included Patrick Henry's "Give me liberty or give me death" speech. He was trying to get across to the students why the speech got people so riled up. The students took copious notes but he realized they did not have the conception of being provoked by a speech. He came up with an idea. He was the director of the theater club and he asked one of the theater students to come into his history class and read what he had written for the class. The boy walked into the class and explained that their teacher would be there in a few minutes but that they were to take notes on the speech he was about to read. The students obliged and the boy proceeded to play the part of the speaker who spoke directly before Patrick Henry who was arguing in favor of a peaceful reconciliation with Britain. Then he finished by saying: "Now representing the other region of Virginia here's Patrick Henry." The history teacher walked in and stood on his desk and in full oratory fashion, from memory, delivered the "Give me Liberty or Give Me Death" speech. At the end of which the students were shouting "Hang the British! Kill them!" They processed the experience, first acknowledging that it was fun to see their teacher jump up on the desk, but also realizing how moved they were by the speech itself and how they truly understood its importance at that time.

Another time in the same unit this same teacher wanted to demonstrate to the students how the American soldiers were able to conquer the British army, deemed the best army in the world at that time. He taught the girls in the class the Continental battle drill: "We took twenty minutes of the class and I said, 'Guys, I want you to sit and watch, I'm going to show you how British soldiers were drilled.' Before I knew it those girls were working like clockwork. They had the first drill down, tamping the powder in their muskets while the second row was firing over their heads." While processing this initial experience the girls indicated that they felt powerful and enjoyed the synchronization of the drill. He sent the girls out in the hall to practice: "Then I turned to the guys and said 'Now I'm George Washington . . . Men the British are advancing on town! They're going to come in here in overwhelming force. Go hide behind anything you can find.' They turned over my desk, they put the lectern on its side, they were hiding behind bookcases. I said, 'Girls advance and fire!' The girls walked in and they looked magnificent. The first row went down on their knees and they fired. I said 'Now what do you have to do?' They started tamping down the powder in the their guns and the second row stood up. I said to the guys, 'Gentlemen, while this first row is reloading their weapons what are you going to do?' They said, 'We're going to shoot them.' That's the idea! They popped up from behind everywhere and starting shooting. Before you knew it we had dead bodies laying all over the floor and the girls are trying to regroup and the guys running around." The students began to understand how it was that a guerilla war might defeat a standard army. This led to some discussion about the Vietnam war. The students got some sense of what it was that was really happening at two different periods of history.

Many teachers agree that imagination has to do with unusualness or uniqueness. One teacher spoke of ways that teachers encourage students to use their imaginations. She tries to get the students to understand that "being individual, being different, is great." She thinks that sometimes students do not feel comfortable with doing something completely different than the others: "For kids to express their imagination, they have to be fairly confident that it's going to be accepted. I think that a teacher has to set up a value system. I want you to be imaginative, I want you to be original, creative and let's show the value in each of those."

Some teachers feel that they need to be more or less imaginative with different groups of students: "Of course you need it more with the younger ones, they need a teacher who can really get in there and keep their attention and you have to change things. So you have to have an imagination." Yet many junior and senior high school teachers will tell you that at their age level is where an imaginative teacher is most essential. It appears to be a universal necessity.

Part of the dictionary (*Webster's Ninth New Collegiate Dictionary* 1987) definition of imagination refers to the ability to confront and deal with a problem. One teacher gave a concrete example of solving a problem, as an example of using her imagination during a teaching situation. They were putting on a production. It was to be an hour long production with the entire fourth grade: "I had children whom I couldn't understand. I didn't know why I couldn't understand them. The music teacher was practicing with another group. She said she spent her whole time trying to get one kid to say an S at the end of a word . . . I was able to take that information and use it with my class, and have them practice saying the whole word . . . I was receptive to the input . . . It occurred to me that my problem was the same as the music teacher described. I knew what to do with the information when I got it . . . I knew what the problem was and I could translate that into a solution that I could then convey to the children. It's imagining." You may find yourself with more mundane problems like making better use of time and space in the classroom. When teaching in a primary classroom, I would allow students considerable work time in various centers throughout the room. It was problematic to get them to clean up the centers in order that we might all gather back together to evaluate and discuss their projects. I found myself wasting valuable time and energy with my use of voice and going from center to center and so on. I imagined an array of possible approaches to solve the problem and came up with a designated sign carrier. I made a simple sign which read "It is clean up time." I had explained to the students that I would choose a responsible person to carry it from center to center and impressed upon them their own responsibility to act upon the sign immediately and then they too may be able to be the sign bearer another day. This simple solution worked well to alleviate a rather troubling problem for me. Certainly the solutions we imagine do not always work. In that case it is time for more imagining down a different course.

One teacher recounted an example from a second grade classroom. In this example she refers to "an imaginative way to teach" as making things fun and interesting for the students. It is important that concepts be made relevant to the students through an experiential context. The class had been working on map skills. She does not believe in "worksheets, busy work and memorizing stuff." She wants the students to experience for themselves: "One of the things that we did was to go outside in the morning and look where the sun was and figure out what was east. Then we moved ourselves around to face other directions. I want to reinforce that north is always north no matter where we are . . ." While planning this "imaginative" lesson, she found herself using another capacity of her own imagination as she envisioned what was needed and thought of how the scenario would be played out in the school setting: "I thought it would be fun to send them on a treasure hunt around the school, having to follow the directions. I have twenty-two kids and they're working with partners so I needed eleven treasure hunts. I spread little slips of paper out on the dining room table last night, saying 'Leave the classroom, turn to the north' and that kind of stuff. I was imagining what it would be like."

Hohler (1982, p. 74) mentions an "intuiting activity of the imagination." He declares that imagination can either be a product of, or can produce this "intuiting activity." One teacher related teaching moments when he had to react spontaneously as his most imaginative kinds of lessons: "I think the moments that stand out in my mind the most, centered around either things that the kids have brought up or some social issues. For example, I was teaching BD (students with behavior disorders) at the time. The day of the shuttle disaster, we were watching the liftoff. Complete devastation. They started talking about loss and death and separation and tragedy . . . I had to be imaginative enough to take all of that in and then on the spot be able to organize it so that I could address it over a period of time. It was a phenomenal experience. We ended that whole segment by writing letters to the families, telling them how we felt . . . I think that was a real teachable moment . . . Not knowing what the students are going to respond to, I need to know how to react and that takes the imagination."

While teaching social studies, another such "teachable moment" arose for this teacher. He was beginning a unit on the Civil War and talking about the division in the country. He was beginning to lead the students through some of the feelings evoked as soldiers left their families to go off to battle: "Divorce was not my idea. It came up when I talked about being left and someone said, 'Yeah, I felt really scared when my folks split up.' Boom! You pick up on the thought." So a teacher's imagination can ignite a student's and in turn the spark is thrown back. Imaginative teachers rely on student feedback and input to enhance their own imaginations and to keep things relevant to the students.

Variation of ways to approach a subject takes imagination on the part of the teacher: "I think sometimes part of the art of teaching is being able to say the same thing in different ways. Whether it be through different media or different words. So they can reach the maximum number of people. Sometimes I do really insane things in my class, no one should ever see them. But it becomes effective." This high school math teacher related a story about her "Friday Fundays." The students are so involved that "they don't even realize they're learning geometry. They think it's just a fun day." The students were given a choice of whether they would like to work on a computer or make a kaleidoscope, a kite or a mobile to hang in the room. There was promise of competitive kite flying for the kite makers and a display of the kaleidoscopes and mobiles. The students enjoyed the alternatives and became quite involved in their projects. Students are using some of their shop time to help construct their kaleidoscopes. This project is being linked to lessons on tessellations. This idea that learning is fun is sadly described as the antithesis of what is expected in the schools by students and teachers in general. This math teacher has jokingly referred to this fun process as tricking the students into learning.

Another teacher agreed with the need to respond to the pleasure of learning. He also comments on the basic lack of enjoyment typically related to the schooling process: "I see imagination as giving in to our sense of fun. Why can't schools be fun? I have a line. It's an unusual day when I don't use it at least once. I turn around and I'll say 'Stop smiling, you're in school now. You are not supposed to be enjoying this.' They laugh all the more at that saying, 'Wait a minute. Why can't this be enjoyable?'"

Imagination is essential to the educative process. A high school communications teacher told me: "It's essential because they're (the students are) imaginative. Listen to their humor, they are tremendously creative . . . To try to teach English without giving them a sense of the wonder and mystery of it, is false. You can't do it. You can teach them grammar and that's important, but you can't teach them to think without using imagination." Imagi-

native teaching is not lecturing, it typically involves looking at how to make something interesting for the students. Imaginative teaching—making concepts "come
alive" for students necessitates engaging them in the
process. There are many techniques for involving the
students. The high school communications teacher says
that sometimes he "will walk in and make an outrageous
statement that I know will immediately put them on the
defensive. I'll walk in and say 'Do you realize that since
women got the right to vote this country has been at
war almost constantly, we've had a depression, and we've
gone through the worst economic times ever? I don't
think we should have done that.' . . . The more engaged
they are in their learning the more they are going to
enjoy it. The more they enjoy it the more they are going
to learn. It's obvious and yet difficult to accomplish."

Sometimes teachers' use of imagination will come
in telling stories to the class and letting them try to experience what is being depicted in the story. One teacher
related the use of story when teaching a unit on the
Alamo: "There are a lot of ways you can teach that. You
can teach it as a story of John Wayne holding off the
dastardly Mexicans. Instead what I did was I turned
down the lights and said let me tell you a story . . . I
told them the story of how the soldiers came to be in
the Alamo." The power of storytelling calls forth the students' imaginations as well. The teacher described in
detail what the interior of the fort looked like, how much
food they had and how many people were there. He then
asked the students to picture themselves as soldiers at
that time and place: ". . . imagine you've just woken up
in the morning and you go out to your guard post and
you see four thousand Mexican soldiers surrounding the
place. How do you feel?" He would then have the students write down their feelings of the moment and then
proceed: "Bowie and Crockett and all the brave people
that were there knew this was the end of the line. And so

what did Travis do? He drew a line in the dirt and he said we have been given a flag of truce. Anybody who wants to leave they can leave now. The Mexicans will give them free passage. They had reason to believe that they probably would be given free passage. Yet nobody stepped over the line. Why not?" The imaginative involvement of the story helped the students to understand events which took place long ago. It made the period in time come alive for the students in the present classroom setting. The students were given a sense of the history rather than mere information and facts.

An imaginative high school English teacher uses alternatives to teach poetry. He will bring in some of the "beat poetry" from the 1950s which will spark some of the students. But one thing he does really engages them all—he will tell the students that they all know poetry quite well: "You could all repeat the lyrics of fifty poems . . . the example I gave was a Bruce Springsteen song . . . This is poetry, Springsteen sits down and lines don't come all the way to the end and sometimes they rhyme and sometimes they don't and they're telling a story." Many of the students do not like the idea of analyzing the song lyrics at first. They argue that there is no underlying meaning, songs are just taken at face value. The English teacher used the example of ". . . a Springsteen song 'Bobby Jean' which is fairly ambiguous. In the song the narrator talks about missing Bobby Jean and 'All the fun we used to have. I went to your house and you're not there anymore.' We read the lyrics of the song. I said okay, if you think you can't analyze this song, if it is 'just what it is' then without talking to anybody else, take out a piece of paper and in the next two minutes write down who Bobbie Jean is, what the relationship between Bobbie Jean and the narrator is, and what happened to Bobbie Jean. We came up with eight different explanations." The students could not agree if Bobbie Jean was a boy or girl, they could not agree if he or she was dead or alive, if they were lovers or not, if they were friends. They came up with a multitude of different solutions. The students demanded the "real" interpretation and many were irritated when the teacher said that they were all valid and that he honestly did not know what the song writer meant in each aspect. The students realized what poetry analysis meant. They got further involved with other pieces and had fun with the process.

Imagination in Curriculum Planning

As one teacher said, "Imagination is picturing in your mind what will transpire or is likely to take place. I think teachers do that when they're planning ahead, making lesson plans." I have touched on the idea of the teacher's use of imagination as they plan for classroom activity. Here we will examine this issue as distinct from the use of the imagination in the classroom. In the previous section I mentioned a teacher who was planning for a treasure hunt to teach map skills. She pictures the class when planning and envisions what she would like the class to do. She feels that her imagination in planning is not always in the sense of visual imagery, but she will often run through dialogues when planning. So there is an element of auditory imaging. I have often used the technique of both auditory and visual imaging when planning for classes. As I previously mentioned, my primary method of planning was that of running a "video" in my mind of what might occur within the confines of particular activities. The video-like images included multi-sensory impressions.

When teachers and I speak of visualization in terms of planning for the day many similar ideas are conjured. Teachers question themselves a lot while planning. A kindergarten teacher iterated some of the questions which might go through her mind as she pictures the class while planning a lesson: "Can I imagine this with forty kids? No . . . can it work with twenty? No. Do I do this on the carpet? What do I need? What has worked in the past? Do I need to change the desks for this kind of situation? Who can sit next to each other? You get the picture of which two kids are there—no, it's not going to work." A high school teacher imagines his separate classes and wonders: "I'll sit down and write the objectives for the day. What is it I want them to learn? What is it I want them to be able to explain or comprehend? Then I'll think what is the best way to get them to that point. How can I teach this in a way so that it is fun but not fun and games? How can I make it so it's interesting but not silly?"

Sometimes questions are posed to oneself after a day's teaching has ended. The evaluation process is inextricably linked to the procedure of planning—it is an ongoing cycle. Teachers imagine the day in retrospect: "I go through the class periods and think: Who didn't I reach? Did I reach the class? Sometimes I start my rehearsal for what I'm going to be doing the next day. Sometimes I think of who I'm going to call that evening to either tell that they've done a terrific job or I was really concerned about something." This is somewhat reminiscent of Schubert's "IMPRO" (1975). As a teacher dialogues with self, the students and the environment, certain curricular decisions are made through deliberation and consideration of possibilities and probabilities.

Of course even when you visualize a new situation, you are not always sure how things may go. With experience the visualizations become more and more realistic, since you often base your imaginings on past events. Management issues are easier to envision as you gain in practice in the classroom.

One teacher paralleled Barell (1980) and Torrance and Myers (1970) regarding the purposefulness and deliberate quality that is needed in creative and imaginative activities, so that students understand that these modes of thought are valued and not frivolous: "You have to realize that in order for an activity to be successful it can't just be imaginative. It has to be realistic and it can't turn out to be a big joke. It can't be a mess . . . the kids aren't going to trust that the next activity that you try to do in that way is going to be successful either." So it is important to plan carefully in a purposeful and pragmatic manner.

A couple of teachers did not view planning as an imaginative activity. One teacher actually opposed the ideas: ". . . classroom management and planning—that's the other side of imagination. That's the real rigid part . . ." Another teacher said of lesson planning: "I consider that an intellectual exercise rather than a visualization or creative exercise." As discussed earlier in the definition chapter, being imaginative is a highly intellectual endeavor. It could be that some teachers do not use visual forms of imagination when planning. One teacher said she does not visualize individual students, but she does look at concepts and how they might relate: "I think of what concept I want to provide them with. And then, how can I relate that concept to something that is interesting, that would be fun for them, that would be familiar to them and that would be effective to them to demonstrate what I want to show."

Other teachers often imagine whole classes at a time. A high school teacher who has five distinct groups of students each day will envision each class separately: "I will sit and think about each of my classes individually, because every class has its own individual character. I will think what approach would work best for them. As I plan, I'll picture what they're doing . . . sometimes I'll picture individual students."

Teachers do not plan lessons only while sitting at their desks in the classroom. Mainly ideas occur when doing other routine activities of the day. Driving is a good time for imaginative lesson planning for many teachers, especially if there is a lengthy commute: "When I'm on my way to work, like today . . . I just imagine the different responses I'm going to get . . . I'm going to imagine that somebody is completely lost. I've got to come up with something . . . I have a lot of ideas of what I'm going to do. I'm not going to do half of them. I've got to make a decision . . . I almost imagine the whole day and just get under my belt different things that I might use given different circumstances. It's visual and it's also auditory. In my mind's eye and ear I can hear and see what's going on."

Much of my own imaginings in planning were analogous to the way this teacher describes his situation. My internal video would run on for me while I was busy doing other mundane activities such as driving, cooking, cleaning or simply relaxing. I would particularly image a lot when planning something new, unusual or different. I would imagine what certain children would do and say. Yes, it was notably similar to video, because not all of imagination is "seeing pictures." I could definitely hear particular student voices. Often my imagined classroom in my inner video would turn on to review the day. Actually this is what I remember most of the video. It was a playback or rerun. These reruns would be vivid with much detail as to what happened with emphasis on what had been said by individuals. Sometimes I would stop the video and rewind to replay certain portions over and over. Once in a while these repetitions had something to do with a little ego boosting as I gloated over wonderful things happening among the kids. But almost as often, the repetitions were about things that did not go exactly right. I yelled at a child. Oh, I would hear that over and over until I knew what I must do—apologize. The replays would give me insight into how I would proceed the next day, thus planning would spawn from the evaluation.

Planning and implementation of daily curricular concepts are inseparable. While most teachers plan out the basics of a lesson, often with contingency plans, so much of what happens in the class is dependent on the interaction. One teacher called her plan her "checklist" which is ever present in her mind while teaching: "Broadly speaking I know what I want to accomplish by the end of a class, but I can't spell it out because the components are going to be so different . . . On that checklist there are concepts . . . The students supply the specifics and then I supply specifics connected to theirs." Many teachers might refer to this as having clear goals in mind. These goals and objectives can be concrete or global in perspective. A teacher spoke of her general "plan" for all teaching—to strive to enhance the consciousness rather than the self-consciousness of the students: "This is what underlies everything I do. I have these various concepts that aid this idea, but to be conscious is to be focused on something outside oneself, but with the consciousness of a self who is doing that. As opposed to self-consciousness whose aim is to perform for somebody else . . . The object of education is to free the self. Alas, too often we go in precisely the opposite direction and make the self twist and turn and be utterly miserable trying to make itself into something else. The freedom of the confidence of the self to be itself . . . is what should be at the base of any curriculum that is taught. Somebody said the aim of a liberal arts education was to teach the 'I' intrinsic in every human statement."

This same teacher sees a relationship between planning and implementation: ". . . you can't separate the two. Yet in a way you can, and you must . . . Planning, the checklist is static . . . Implementation is the willingness to trust that checklist, trust that you know that checklist . . . Then you're just going to do whatever will arise that day . . . My checklist goes like this (shows straight line) and my implementation goes like this (shows random movement). I must have the courage never to know where it's going to go . . . But I must have my checklist."

Do you visualize when planning lessons? Is the planning process a creative or imaginative process itself? How do you do your best planning?

Intuition in the Classroom

In the previous section I alluded to the spontaneous reality of the classroom setting. Plans are made, but most often the teacher's intuitive judgment takes over in the moment-to-moment course of the school day. This section is meant to clarify some of the connotations attached to intuition in teaching.

One teacher who feels that she is more intuitive in the classroom than she is imaginative, refers to teaching as a conversation: "You get messages all the time. It's a constant conversation." When discussing the philosophy of phenomenology, as it applies to teaching, Kneller (1984, p. 44) states that "Merleau-Ponty also tells me that teaching is a conversation . . . even the most sophisticated conversation relies on intonation, gesture, and expression." Communication with students allows for subtle intuitions as teachers "read" aspects of the interaction. One teacher says that this is not specifically inherent to teaching and likens these intuitions to feelings that anyone gets when conversing with another: "I think teaching is really a communication . . . You have to make eye contact with the children . . . You have to try to see what is happening with them . . . It's often a non-verbal interaction. You have to be able to tune into that. For instance in my class I can *feel* the mood of the class. I don't think it's any different than when meeting somebody. You get a feeling if the person likes you or not. When I met you I felt I liked you, and you probably got good vibes from me. It's the same thing, you can feel if somebody's open towards you . . . But the big difference is, again, you're doing it with thirty at a time."

Quite a few teachers have voiced the difference between teaching lessons, subject matter or curricula as opposed to teaching students. Being in tune with the students is paramount in good teaching. It is through this empathy that intuitions are manifested. Many teachers believe that this is something that evolves with experience and confidence: ". . . most times student teachers have big problems because they teach a lesson, they don't teach children. They're so involved with themselves—will I remember this? did I cover that point?" Hopefully we all improve through further experiences of our own. We can also increase our understanding through the experience of others. We all have intuitive ability. Louis Rubin (1985, p. 61) agrees that intuition is an integral aspect of teaching and that it is not arcane: "Intuition is essential in teaching, moreover, because much instruction involves monitoring and appraising learner understanding. No special clairvoyance is needed to discern that a child is having trouble."

The use of intuition in the classroom can take on distinct modalities. One such mode is the ability to "wing it" or spontaneously alter one's plan in a given situation. Teachers refer to having to totally disregard their original plans because situations do not always go according to what is expected. Occasionally emergency situations arise, sometimes the mood in the classroom is something that has not been anticipated. The classroom is a fluid environment. Teachers each have or quickly acquire the ability to "think on their feet" and to "switch gears" at a moments notice. Knowing or feeling the right tack to take at the spur of the moment is often referred to as having an intuitive insight.

Another intuitive mode I have mentioned is the process of "reading the students." One teacher said it was necessary to objectively look at yourself while you are teaching to help "pick up on" cues from the students: "I think you almost have to be two people. You're the one conducting the lesson, but then you're also the one observing it all . . . If you can stand outside and critique yourself while you're doing it, you become more effective at whatever it is you do. With kids it's usually a kind of puzzled look that tells you they're not understanding. With adults their body language is so explicit . . . I can tell by their faces if I'm going way too fast or if what I'm suggesting is not their style or that kind of thing. Then I slow down or take another tack."

Good teachers respond intuitively to student behavior: "Intuitive reaction in the classroom is aroused by an expression on a face, a wiggly wave of unrest, the way a question is asked or perhaps by the absence of a question or indication of curiosity." So often it is not merely doing an about face and changing the course of a lesson entirely, it is fine tuning and making slight alterations on the spot that can make the difference between student comprehension and apathy. One teacher described this strategy metaphorically: "In a classroom situation it is fun for me to teach often as though it were a fencing exhibition—left, right, forward, back, forward again—thrust! . . . You can ask a question. You get a response. If the question is right, or whatever you do is right to evoke a response, the response should be broader and deeper . . . The intuition is when to change the depth or scope of your question or your example . . . the longer I have taught, it is much easier for me to recognize when to step back, to reverse to give another example, then to go forward."

Many good teachers rarely sit while teaching, especially when addressing a whole class. They need to see all students in order to keep in tune with how each student is responding. The need for eye contact is essential: "Most of what I do, though, is based on eye contact. You notice, when I teach I never sit, I stand. I'm greatly dependent on visual feedback from the kids. I have to be able to see their faces. Body language is important . . . After a while when you teach, it really stands out."

Reading the students and shifting to match energy levels and particular student needs are all regarded as essential aspects of teaching. Many teachers recognize intuition as an integral facet of teaching: "First of all any good teacher has to use their intuition constantly or they are not a good teacher . . . Intuition comes in looking at students and reading their body language, getting to know them, understanding where they're at and respecting where they're at."

Unfortunately, due to the structure of most schools, teachers sometimes feel inhibited from reacting as spontaneously as they would like. This is more often felt by high school teachers who are locked into class schedules for relatively shorts periods of time. One high school teacher mentioned that this is sometimes a frustration: "You're not allowed to react as spontaneously as you would like. There are times when I'd love to take my class outside, or do things quickly. But because of the necessity of scheduling and student safety you're not able to do it."

Being open to your own intuition as a teacher can assist you with how you teach the entire class. Any teacher will tell you that something that worked well once will not necessarily work the same way the next time you try it. Often intuitive insights lead teachers to make appropriate choices based on the sensed mood of the class as a whole: "Intuitively, you begin to understand that some days one approach is just not going to work. Whereas other days it's going to work wonderfully. Some days you can tease your students, and some days you can't. Some days I have to be strict, and stern, and some days I don't have to be that way."

So, intuitively you may know how best to handle a group on different days based on the temperament of the class. But most often teachers rely on their intuitive abilities when relating with individuals within the class: ". . . teachers have to be constantly aware that they've got thirty or thirty-five lives in front of them in any given moment. Many of which are in divergent places."

One of the commonalties I have observed in good teachers is the way they really *look* at their students while teaching. We are reminded, here of the origins of the word intuition, *intueri*, to look upon. Many teachers move right up to the student with whom they are conversing. When speaking to the whole class they are maintaining eye contact with individuals. In this sense they all "teach students, not material," as many teachers put it. In teaching, the subject matter becomes secondary to the learners. Thus, a major part of daily teaching is necessarily spontaneous and intuitive as teachers concern themselves with the of-the-moment needs of the learners.

How do you use your intuition when you teach? Can you think of examples of when you instinctualy knew what to do about an unexpected occurrence in the classroom? Are there times when you have a "gut feeling" that something will or will not work as planned? Do you sometimes look at your students and just know what they are thinking? How often have you altered or totally rejected your original plan for a lesson and simply "winged it" because "it just seemed like the right thing to do?" How do you make spur-of-the-moment decisions in the classroom? Do you use your intuition more than your imagination or vice versa?

In Part II I have considered how teachers' imagination and intuition is manifest in daily classroom activity. This part of the book has set the stage by explaining the terms in reference to teaching and further clarifying their meanings as understood within the context of classroom life. Chapter 4, in particular, has opened the window to various teachers' classrooms to peer at their professional lives and to hear what they have to say about their use of imagination and intuition.

Imaginative stories abound. The idea of intuition is more elusive and, as has been mentioned, notions of intuition are more difficult to verbalize. Therefore stories told regarding intuition are often more succinct as well as less abundant. Intuitive moments by their nature are brief, so understandably the accounts of these instances will be concise as well.

Now that the window is open, I continue to survey the teachers' everyday use of imagination and intuition through my own and other teachers' stories as well as related accounts found in educational literature.

PART III

THEMATIC THREADS
UNRAVELED

*I have here only made a nosegay of culled flow-
ers, and have brought nothing of my own but
the thread that ties them together.*

—Michel Eyquem de Montaigne,
Essays, book III, chapter 11

In the previous chapter, while examining some of
the ways teachers use their imagination and intuition,
several general themes were emerging. As I talk with
teachers regarding these occurrences I find many more
themes apparent. As I grapple with these elusive phenomena in order to make more sense of them for myself,
other teachers and students, I find the discussion of
such themes valuable. In this part we will examine some
of the threads which can be unraveled from the interwoven complexity of teachers' everyday use of imagination
and intuition.

Although we need to look at the whole picture to
understand something in context, it is often helpful to
dissect elements for closer inspection. Examining the
complexities of the individual fibers of a cloth can deepen

our appreciation for the overall texture and intricacy of the rewoven fabric. If you see how the tapestry is put together, you are better able to understand how to make your own. Good ideas are valuable resources meant to be unfurled in our individual attempts to weave imaginative and intuitive classroom fabrics of our own.

CHAPTER 5

FREE TO BE

The element of freedom is inherent in imaginative and intuitive teaching. The use of one's imagination can be a freeing experience—letting go of existing boundaries to examine possibilities, endless possibilities. Alternately one needs a certain amount of freedom in order to be imaginative. School administrators can set the tone necessary to allow teachers to feel free enough to use their imaginations to the fullest when planning and implementing exciting and meaningful learning experiences for the students. This might mean a higher noise level at times, slightly disheveled classrooms and an occasional alteration in class time and location. Administrators who welcome, or at least tolerate such behavior can make teachers feel freer to explore new educational vistas as they envision interesting experiences in response to the needs and desires of the students.

As a teacher you need to allow yourself to be free enough to listen to your intuitive voice when reacting to students in the classroom and planning meaningful activities for them. The external freedom or restrictions of the school setting are often areas teachers have little control over, however you can enhance your own inner sense of freedom. Even in the strictest school, you have a multitude of options within your own classroom.

This chapter examines some themes associated with the idea of freedom as it relates to the teacher's use of imagination and intuition, including: spontaneity, openness, confidence, experience, trust and familiarity.

Why is it necessary to have a sense of freedom in the classroom? Is teaching a spontaneous activity? How open should a classroom setting be? Do you have to be a confident, self-assured person in order to be able to teach effectively? How might experience help a teacher? In what ways do familiarity and trust pave the way for imaginative and intuitive teaching?

Spontaneity and Openness

> *How do I work? I grope.*
>
> —Albert Einstein

The element of spontaneity is intrinsic to many definitions of intuition. So much of the teaching day is unpredictable. An imaginative teacher learns to use what occurs in the spur of the moment as a key to unlocking imaginative learning in the students. Much learning occurs spontaneously during lessons due to an intuitive teacher's response to particular students or the whole class or sometimes to unplanned occurrences. Teachers often spontaneously encourage imaginative connections in the minds of their students due to an intuitive response to what is currently happening in the classroom. During my conversations with teachers regarding intuition, many of them stated that they often spontaneously evaluate a lesson while it is progressing to see if it can be fine tuned or possibly needs to be more drastically altered. There is some educational research of teachers thinking-in-action (Elbaz 1983; Haley-Oliphant 1987), which alludes to the spontaneous nature of such reflection in the middle of a lesson. Teachers mention that they often "go with" their feelings. You need to be monitoring yourself while you are teaching. As one elementary teacher put it: "You're the one conducting the lesson, but then you're also the one observing it all." Many of us have that experience while teaching, spontaneously reviewing the situation and making adjustments. It seems to be a process of the imagination to be able to observe yourself while you are performing.

Spontaneous decisions are continually required of teachers in any classroom situation. Teachers must constantly reflect and monitor the ongoing events of classroom life. A teacher referred to this as "editing" or making "split-second decisions." This is an appropriate demeanor for any good teacher. One teacher said that spontaneous evaluation is her dominant mode of assessment: "Sometimes I'll say to the kids 'Uh-uh, this is not going to work today. We will come back to this tomorrow.' Right then and there. If I don't know right then, while it's happening, I won't know later. I have to be open to see them (cues) so I can know what to do."

Schon believes that dealing with situations spontaneously is an integral aspect of many professional lives. Practitioners are continually reflecting, reevaluating and conducting "on-the-spot-experiment(s)" (Schon 1983, p. 62). Schon refers to the "intermittent zones of practice" or uncertain circumstances as a swamp that all practitioners need to wade through to cull the relevance lurking there. As one spontaneously gleans insight from this intermittent zone, the uncertainty of the situation is transformed and gives rise to an element of certitude, thus bolstering the confidence of the reflective practitioner. In relation to classroom situations, teachers need to remain open to the possibilities that lie in this realm of uncertainty and flexible enough to wade through the dubious swamp without being pulled down by it.

Noddings and Shore (1984, p. 53) allude to "the clarity and certainty with which intuitive knowledge affects us." The threads of "spontaneity" and "confidence" are intertwined here. Confidence emerges from the spontaneous certainty and lucid direction this assurance offers. Conversely, it could also be said that the feeling of spontaneous clarity and certainty is attained through confidence. In the midst of a spontaneous deliberation it is often difficult to explain why one feels so certain of the appropriateness of the decision. Even later after having time to ponder and reflect on the situation, it is often difficult to verbalize why one has had this perception of absolute certainty. It may have been "just a gut feeling."

Spontaneity is one of the attributes which I attach to my definition of intuition. In a rudimentary way intuition or perception is a spontaneous occurrence. This may be something that inspires the imagination. The imagination appears to be something that one needs in order to be able to work at enhancing or further developing the perception or insight. Metaphorically, intuition is the spontaneous spark and imagination fans the fire until it blazes to fruition. Intuition may spontaneously disclose an idea but it takes an active imagination to bring the idea to life—to make it happen—to be reality.

Classroom settings have certain properties that distinguish them from other environments. Unpredictability and the constant press for immediate action (Doyle 1986) are two such characteristics. The need for openness and a willingness, on the part of the teacher, to "go with the flow" is critical to interactive and imaginative classroom settings. Haley-Oliphant (1987) refers to an unpredictable "of the moment" format in the classroom that she studied. Since the teacher of this classroom uses open-ended questions with the students and there are no right answers, students are propelled into a state of wonder. The teacher goes with them on this "wonder-full" journey, constantly acting and reacting in a spontaneous manner. Another teacher I talked to feels that "just going with the hunch, and saying this is going to go right now," is often the most important thing that a teacher can do.

Interwoven with the theme of spontaneity is the theme of openness. A liberated teacher can instill the attributes of openness and freedom in her students in the classroom. Why is being open important to intuition? One teacher answers: "Because intuition at its core isn't rational. Its nothing you can put your finger on. So the logical mind has a tendency to reject intuition as being superstitious, hunches, so on, and so forth. Whereas an open person says there must be a reason I feel this way, let's go with it and explore it. So I think openness to yourself and to your students is the key part of it." Being open to yourself allows you to sense those subtle feelings which let you know when something is needed. Being open with your students is critical to all other aspects of teaching. It paves the way for sharing, trusting, caring and all meaningful interaction.

Open communication is essential in any good relationship. The continual "conversation" of teaching requires an open give and take on the part of teachers and students. One teacher says she needs to be open in order to "read" the students to discern the subtle cues and needed feedback to know how to continue. She, along with others insist that you can "feel" when someone is not understanding completely or having a problem. You can "just tell" that a student is concealing information or that another is being totally honest. It is important to keep the lines of communication open within the classroom. Some teachers refer to this as being open enough to feel and respond to the "vibes" from the students. Some teachers speak of being open and "cuing in" to the energy level of their classes as an intuitive way of understanding how to proceed with a learning experience. Many teachers purposely develop an open setting in their classrooms, where students feel free to make choices and carry on discussion with peers and the teacher. Good teachers agree that an open atmosphere is essential to allow for meaningful interaction to occur.

Being open implies being free. Sutherland (1971) suggests that teachers ought to allow students the "freedom to think" thus encouraging students to use their imaginations. Teachers must have their own sense of freedom before they can really provide opportunities that promote their students' imaginations. Teachers certainly need an inner sense of freedom to be open enough for imaginative and intuitive endeavors. It is also beneficial to be granted external freedom through approval of supervisors and other powers that be. As I mentioned at the onset of this chapter, the administration needs to encourage imaginative teaching. Similarly, students need their teacher's approval to feel free enough to stretch their imaginations. Sometimes students prefer to conform and follow the lead of peers rather than to try using their own imaginations. Teachers need to recognize this student who does not feel free enough to be unique and provide special encouragement. One teacher proposed that it may be more necessary for experienced teachers to open up to new approaches and innovative ideas to incorporate in their teaching.

What does being "open" in the classroom mean to you? Are you open to spontaneous occurrences?

Confidence and Experience

> *The mutual confidence on which all else depends can be maintained only by an open mind and a brave reliance upon free discussion.*
>
> —Learned Hand from Speech to the Board of Regents, University of the State of New York (1952).

Confidence is a significant issue related to the teacher's use of imagination and intuition in daily classroom activities. Teachers might have intuitive feelings, but unless they have a sense of confidence they will not be able to fully use the insight or react sincerely to their intuition. In relation to the preceding section, the inner feeling of freedom to be open and spontaneous is greatly enhanced by a sense of confidence in oneself.

In chapter 4 I mentioned a teacher who refers to having an imagined "checklist" in mind while teaching: "the more confidence I get as a teacher the more the checklist is in my unconscious," hence promoting a freer, more spontaneous classroom performance. This same teacher also explains that when a teacher does not feel this sense of confidence, the insecurity can manifest itself into fear rather than freedom with a resulting lack of imagination in the teaching process. She depicts such unproductive teaching caused by "a complete lack of ego," a time of anxiety when one's sense of determination is unnerved. During such a time there is a lack of communication with oneself as well as others. It is as if this connection is buried, "like snow drifting over." When one is not in conversation with oneself, if one has lost confidence, there can be no creativity and imagination.

Too often, beginning teachers allow a lack of confidence to turn to fear and hesitate to plan creative experiences which they are not sure they can control. A teacher's lack of confidence is related to her lack of connection to the "fullness of things." At such lonely times a teacher might tend to blame many external things for the emptiness she is feeling. One teacher said: "What happens to me, when I feel that cut off from the connectedness to the fullness of things, I feel frightened inside . . . I don't know how to proceed. When I get into that shape anything that I do is governed by fear, rather than by confidence . . . I think that we are a fear-driven profession. We're afraid of everything. We put it all outside. We call it anarchy of the kids. We call it not being able to keep order. We call it not being able to motivate." We need to recognize when we get into that state and ask ourselves "why?" Why am I afraid to try this with my class? There may be some legitimate reasons. Then again it could be a lack of confidence on my part which I may want to explore.

Schon (1983) refers to a practitioner's loss of confidence in line with loss of control and competence. He calls this the "zone of coming apart." This is a state in which the practitioner is vulnerable and defensive, and as the one teacher put it, "governed by fear." It is the opposite of fear, it is the confidence that spurs a teacher on to imaginative teaching.

Confidence is an integral aspect of the use of intuition. One teacher's definition of intuition includes the themes of confidence and spontaneity: "It's the feeling of confidence to go with something that just occurs to you spontaneously. It probably isn't as spontaneous as it might appear. I don't really think you can be intuitive until you've had some experience, felt some confidence. So you feel safe enough to take a risk and just do something spontaneously."

Confidence is inherent to teachers' use of intuition in the classroom. Sometimes you may find yourself being guided by subtle feelings telling you how to proceed because you have confronted similar circumstances in the past and because you know your students so well. Often these insights are a result of having reflected on a similar situation in the classroom. The knowledge that you have made sound spontaneous decisions in the past enhances your confidence in this ability and facilitates further use of intuition.

Intuition is based in prior knowledge. It has to do with your awareness of and sensitivity to the knowledge gained through past experience regarding various circumstances, your own feelings, different people, interactions, responses and routines. The continual insights or subtle feelings we get to guide us through lessons and other educational endeavors depend on an extensive storehouse of information. The more data that we have accumulated through past experiences, the more reliable our intuitive feelings will be. As our teaching experience grows and we continue to utilize our intuitions we come to appreciate the accuracy of these subtle guides. This, in turn, bolsters our confidence in these intuitive feelings and in ourselves, which, in turn, causes us to have more and more insights which we feel secure enough to utilize, and so on—it is a vitalizing spiral effect.

Rubin (1985, p. 61) also encourages teachers to have confidence in their intuitive feelings. He explains that these insights are easily acquired through experience. As explained in chapter 2, his term "artist teacher" is similar to what I have been calling an imaginative, intuitive teacher:

> Make use of intuition and hunch in modifying routine *practices*. Artist teachers who seem, so often, to do exactly the right thing at exactly the right time have well-tempered instincts. They use insight, acquired through long experience, to get at the heart of a matter and sense what will work. They not only prefer to obey these instincts but are uneasy when, for some reason, they must disregard them. Such teachers find instinctive knowledge exceedingly useful, readily accessible, and an effective shortcut in reaching conclusions.

Rubin tells us that as teachers gain experience they can "sharpen their intuitive faculties and use them more fully. After a few years in the classroom, sophistication increases, there is a greater sensitivity to the problems of pedagogy, and the subtleties of the art gradually become more clear" (Rubin 1985, p. 62).

Teaching is only one aspect of our lives as human beings. However, teaching encompasses so much of life.

When we grow as a person we grow as a teacher. The more our personal confidence flourishes, the more comfortable we are with ourselves and our lives, the more we are able to positively affect the lives of others. Part of a philosophy of life which can lead to enriched teaching includes awareness and appreciation of one's own insights, confidence in those intuitive feelings, and willingness to act upon them.

In referring to a spontaneous decision to alter an activity, a teacher mentioned the fact that such a quick change requires some confidence that comes with experience: "I think as a beginning teacher I probably would have struggled through that original plan and tried to make the best of it. I think that a not very good teacher would have blamed the kids for not understanding or finishing in time. But really the concept was beyond them." As a more experienced teacher, she now had the confidence to stop an activity and stir it in a different direction.

One teacher feels that part of her development as a teacher, as she grew more confident, was to be less imposing on the students: "I think back to when I had the view of the teacher as the one who knew it all and who was going to impart it to the unknowing. I wanted to do it in entertaining ways. I remember performing and manipulating them. Now I view the teacher as a facilitator. You take the kid from wherever he or she is. I'm not imposing as much as I used to. I thought that I had the right answers before. Now I don't really think that I've got the answers, just the questions." Another teacher expressed similar views. In lacking confidence the teacher's tendency is to blame the students for the feeling of fear and for not knowing how to proceed. She feels that an important step in becoming a good teacher is being able "to make the shift."

"The shift" she referred to is moving away from the feeling that the teacher is the one who has all the right answers imparting the knowledge to the students to: "two people on a path together, the kid and the teacher." This shift comes with experience. But sometimes when the teacher's confidence is unnerved by something or she is feeling defensive, even an accomplished veteran teacher may resort to playing "God." A teacher said: "It's difficult for all of us. I stub my toes on that frequently. I don't stay there very often, but if a kid asks me something and I don't know an answer, most of the time I am pretty free to say 'I don't know. Let's find out.' But sometimes, if I'm uptight that day, I'll flip into my old mode of what a teacher's supposed to do and I'll panic because I don't know the answer."

A veteran teacher of thirty years who appears confident and self-assured in the classroom confessed that every autumn she has some hesitation: "I have to tell you every September, before we start, I am sure I cannot teach. I panic. I don't know what I'm going to do, because I think 'Will I still have it?' And I don't know that." Most teachers do not lose confidence that drastically, but it does ebb and flow. It is not uncommon to feel unsure of oneself when starting with a new class, even after having gained much confidence the previous year. The unknown has always carried along with it an element of fear. You can turn the extra energy generated by the anxiety into constructive potential. After consoling a student teacher once with what I thought were reassuring words that she would feel more confident as she gained experience, she wanted to know what she could do in the meantime. I told her to "fake it." Pretending to feel confident can quickly turn to reality as good classroom experiences mount in your memory. What do you do when you are not feeling as confident as you might like?

The feeling of openness is directly linked to the idea of confidence. Many teachers express the opinion that they have been more open to rely on their intuitions as they have gained more confidence through experience.

One teacher said that she was more insecure as a novice teacher but "I've been able to open up to the interaction."

Many teachers speak of an increase in one's intuitive ability as one gains experience and confidence. As one teacher put it: "You get much better at improvising on the spot and thinking of examples and counter examples and bringing people in and going away from your lesson plan and coming back to it and moving in another direction. It is fantastic! . . . you have finally achieved the ability to roam all over and pick up on things as they come. I think it takes a very secure person in the classroom and I don't think new teachers are ever that secure when they first start." Some beginning teachers are obviously more confident than others. And certainly some people's innate intuitive abilities are more acute than others. It does make sense, however, that confidence is enhanced by experience. For many teachers confidence and experience have sharpened their intuitive abilities. One teacher said: "My intuition, I think, has sharpened greatly. I can look at a kid and pretty much understand where he's coming from . . . I think intuition is pretty much a guidance for your decision-making and my decision-making, of course, becomes much better as the years go on."

Some of this expansion of intuitive ability stems from general life experience and getting to know yourself better. Besides an increased awareness of repeated patterns of behavior in others, you improve in your ability to recognize these in yourself. As you come to appreciate your own awareness of energy level, sense of perspective, humor and so on, you "just know" when it is the right time and mood for certain activities and when particular experiences will work best. Life experience increases your confidence in general and you can use that in your teaching. As one teacher put it: ". . . it is more than confidence in your teaching ability, it's confidence in yourself as a person that you can handle the response that you're going to get."

While teachers tend to agree that their intuitive ability increases with experience, a few were not sure that the imaginative aspect also expanded. One teacher even went so far as to say he thought he might have been more imaginative when he was a less experienced teacher. He felt that he was less inhibited previously. Another teacher who has also found an increase in intuitive ability with experience, fights the idea of becoming less imaginative. He has found many positive aspects to increased confidence in teaching: "The intuition is heightened definitely, just from the experience of it. The imagination, I can see where many people would run into a problem with that. It's easy to get into doing the same things that were done. One way I try to avoid that is I love talking with other teachers and sharing ideas . . . I really try to force myself to stay as open as possible. The more open you stay the more the imagination is going to come. The older I've gotten, I've gotten to be a better teacher." Many teachers grow more imaginative as they gain experience. Teachers often deliberately enhance the creative aspects of their jobs by taking interesting classes and workshops to spark ideas or to gain more confidence with particular methods which will allow for more creativity. The sharing of ideas with colleagues is an excellent way to stoke the fire of the imagination. To many, the use of their imagination is so essential to teaching that it is the only way they know and it just keeps getting better and better.

The idea of having confidence in one's intuitions and trusting these spontaneous insights has been discussed. Trusting in yourself and your abilities as a teacher is an essential aspect of good teaching. But just as important is the element of trust and confidence that the students place in their teacher. Many teachers feel strongly that good teaching cannot occur without the students' trust. Good teachers create the climate for trust within a caring atmosphere. One teacher warns against being intimidating to students: "the power that teachers have to be threatening is enormous, much more so than many realize." He is careful to make things comfortable for the students. His openness with students allows for the trust to naturally occur. This open, trusting climate often leads into social-emotional areas of his students' personal lives. He is often sought out by students as the person whose shoulder they can cry on or the adult they turn to for advice. Due to this trusting, open environment he creates in the classroom, students eagerly engross themselves in the activities he plans.

Genuine care and concern on the part of the teacher can be felt by the students. Students are willing to put their trust in a teacher who they know is concerned about and supportive of them. You earn the trust of your students with sincere effort and competent teaching. How do you know when the students trust you? How do you build a trusting environment?

In what ways does experience enhance your intuitive abilities? Are you more imaginative as you gain experience in teaching? How has your confidence increased?

Familiarity

> *New things are made familiar, and familiar things are made new.*
>
> —Samuel Johnson in Lives of the Poets (1779-1781), Pope.

Some facets of the thematic thread of "familiarity" spawn from the idea of "experience." As a teacher accrues experience, she also increases her familiarity with various elements of teaching: the classroom setting, routines, subject matter, interactions, the diversity of students, their habits, mannerisms, how they think, her own deportment and manner of responding to the students, etc.

Rubin (1985, p. 65) explains that "intuitive thinking . . . is a part of ordinary intelligence, crystallized and sharpened by experience." We become familiar with people and situations through our experience with them. As we gain familiarity through experience our intuitive capabilities are sharpened. These intuitions or perceptions we get accumulate in our storehouse of remembered experiences. Therefore when we are in similar situations, insights occur more quickly:

> As familiarity in a repetitive endeavor accumulates, our intuitive capacities are refined through practice. And as we become familiar with typical situations, we recognize similar patterns. Thus, through stored insight, we often can accelerate the judgmental process by taking advantage of cognitive step-savers. (Rubin 1985, p. 65)

A teacher referred to this "storehouse" or reservoir of knowledge from which teachers "draw upon at given moments in day-to-day teaching." It is familiarity with the circumstances and the students that facilitates what he calls making "split-second decisions." Indeed, it is the facet of familiarity, gleaned from experience, which enables teachers to act and react spontaneously in classroom situations.

It is essential that teachers familiarize themselves with many aspects of their students lives so that they can facilitate connection making and offer relevant contexts for students. By being familiar with and truly understanding their students as individuals teachers can encourage helpful connections in the minds of their students, thereby enhancing imaginative teaching.

A beginning point would be to familiarize yourself with the capabilities of students at the age level you are presently teaching. I tell student teachers that it is essential for them to be able to think like a third grader, or seventh grader, or whatever level they are teaching. When she understands the child's perspective, the teacher is able to provide relevant contexts and encourage meaningful connections for the students. A fourth grade teacher said: "I understand what a fourth grader is like. I can visualize, imagine what their day is like for them. It's a recognition of what their life is like." This teacher is using her imaginative and intuitive capabilities toward compassionate understanding of her students. Here we see the threads of "familiarity" and "caring" entangled. Noddings (1984, p. 16) considers such acknowledgment as an empathic mode of caring as well as understanding:

> Apprehending the other's reality, feeling what he feels as nearly as possible, is the essential part of caring from the view of the one-caring. For if I take on the other's reality as possibility and begin to feel its reality, I feel, also, that I must act accordingly; that is, I am impelled to act as though in my own behalf, but in behalf of the other.

This empathic sensitivity is enhanced through understanding the idiosyncrasies of different age groups in order to respond to them intuitively. Knowledge of basic child development and psychology can aid teachers in their quest to be more sympathetic toward the age level of students they are teaching. A junior high teacher told me: "How I respond to 6th graders is completely different than my intuitive reactions to 8th graders." Of course no two groups are completely analogous, even within the same age range. It is essential to understand the particular students you are teaching. Each class takes on its own personality as a mesh of the individual characters that comprise it.

A high school teacher spoke of the importance of recollecting what it was like to be a high school student and retaining that recollection while planning classroom activities. Kneller (1984, p. 44) agrees with this point because "teaching is an intensely personal experience." A teacher's intuition is enhanced through the memory of what it was like to be a student. This type of recollection strengthens empathy and familiarity with students. Kneller (1984, p. 44) relates that this can influence teachers' responses to be more spontaneous: "As a teacher, I must be in touch with my own past, especially with my earlier perceptions and concepts, which are the source of my strongest emotions. This is the only way I can respond fully and spontaneously to my students and help them deepen the curiosity, elan, and sense of identity inherited from early childhood. The life of reason develops against a background of prereflective experience. If I divorce myself from this background, I become arid and unable to convey the intellectual excitement I would like to feel."

It is crucial to familiarize yourself with each class and how they behave as a group. But I can not stress enough the importance of getting to know your students as individuals. Many teachers feel that this individual familiarity is at the heart of the subtle intuitions they have while teaching. As one teacher puts it, intuition "comes from getting to know the kids over a period of time. The intuition comes in from knowing what my students look like, knowing how they sound, knowing how they dress, knowing how they react. Knowing what makes them laugh or doesn't make them laugh. Really being in tune with them. Paying attention to them as people not as students of thirty, but as individuals in a class."

Good teachers tend to pay attention to the individuals in their class and work with them on a one to one or small group basis more than teaching solely to the whole group. A teacher was speaking to me about facilitating meaningful connections for students. She believes that it is necessary to understand children as individuals in order to be able to personalize the context: "It's imaginative to make connections, therefore it's important to get to know each child as an individual. They're all so different. That's another reason for not doing a lot of whole group instruction . . . Better to meet with them in small groups or individually so you can relate it to them on a personal level."

A teacher's familiarity of subject matter profoundly affects the teacher's intuitive thinking with regard to the particular area of expertise. Familiarity with a subject can lead to making pertinent correlations for yourself and your students within the specific field of study as well as meaningful connections with other subject areas. If you are thoroughly familiar with an area of study you can generate meaningful contexts to enhance student understanding. One high school teacher views this type of intuitive connection-making as leading to imaginative teaching: "If a person is able to make liaisons within his major field as well as among others, then this person has the tools for imaginative presentation."

Familiarity of subject matter is significant for students as well as teachers. It is important when imparting new information to students to continually refer to what is already familiar to them, in order that they might make their own pertinent correlations. New concepts can be evolved from familiar ones so as to keep a relevant context and make sense for the students. The same high school teacher labels this type of teaching from what is known to the unfamiliar as "seed planting." It is important to evoke that familiar knowledge for students as they are being introduced to a new, related concept. As I tell teachers in workshops and classes, it gives the students a familiar "place to hang it on." Without calling up the prior knowledge, new ideas and concepts can "go right over their heads." With a familiar place to put it, there is more of a chance the new information might be retained because it will make sense within a context with which they are already familiar.

Along a similar line of thought, one teacher referred to "the miracle of doing it again." Often when confronted with something new, initially we have no context in which to place it. However, the next time we encounter an analogous circumstance or concept, it has become a little more familiar and we have something in our experiential background with which we can make a connection. The teacher was referring to an instinctive, imaginative way of doing things when she related her ideas regarding this "again" phenomenon: "There's a very tricky shift from having people just do things, to having people being conscious of what they're doing so that they can do them again . . . But this particular process is at the heart of all learning . . . in creating something, first you do it, then you become conscious of what you're doing . . . you haven't integrated the two yet. You've got either spontaneity or otherwise a rather constricted trying to do it again . . . Later, when you're ready, it will integrate . . . all of a sudden you've got it."

Think of any time when you have been learning something for the first time, in history, philosophy, math or any subject. When you first encounter something you may not be able to relate to it, especially if you are simply reading about it by yourself and you have no one immediately available with whom to discuss it. You may not have a context in which to connect to it. So your starting point is often going to have to be this bit of information in isolation. Then as you work through the book, text, article or whatever it is, by the end of a first reading you should have at least the beginning of a frame of reference of a context. If you read it again you would be putting these things that you were learning in relation to each other. Because now you know the context.

The college music history teacher said: "I think of a guy who wrote a wonderful book called *Music is Metaphor*, talking about 'da, da, da, dum' (first four notes of Beethoven's Fifth Symphony). If you've never heard those four notes before, what happens, cumulatively each time you hear those four notes throughout the movement, is there are a thousand agains in that one movement. So by the time you've listened to the movement all the way through one time, the next time you listen you're going to know about 'da, da, da, dum'. That's going to make your listening experience totally different. It's the same with history, or geography, or whatever." Repetition, doing it again, making new things familiar is a major portion of educational endeavors. There is some magic in the insight that happens when a new concept becomes familiar enough to connect and make sense.

Are you more intuitive with a familiar class? How do you imaginatively teach a familiar aspect of a subject?

Implications

The thematic threads of connections, context, confidence, experience, trust and familiarity are so intricately woven that when we attempt to unravel them for inspection they become entangled in some areas where the knots cannot be undone. It is through experience that we gain familiar contexts in which we are able to make meaningful connections. Familiarity accrued through experience bolsters our confidence and permits us to rely on our insights and intuitions.

One of the implications in the discussions in this chapter has been that intuition is enhanced by these facets. Noddings and Shore (1984, p. 64), in the section of their book on "Intuition and Familiarity," inform us of the cyclical process of strengthening intuition. They explain that intuitive understandings within a subject area are usually precipitated by a person's familiarity with the discipline: "Generally, the people most knowledgeable in an area are those who have the most frequent and the most reliable intuitions" (1984, p. 64). However, they caution that being familiar with particular subject matter does not necessarily lead to intuitions. Also there are some people "who exhibit a marvelous intuitive grasp of subject matter in which they are relatively untrained" (Noddings and Shore 1984, p. 65). In addition, Noddings and Shore (1984, p. 65) indicate that while familiarity does intensify intuition, they also think that "intuition may be exercised to develop familiarity. Clearly, if intuition follows, it also leads, and indeed, we have claimed that it provides the very foundation for experience."

In a section of their book, called "Acquiring Familiarity," Noddings and Shore (1984, p. 137) parallel the previously mentioned idea of "seed planting" with students, although they do not label it as such. They develop this idea further and put "an emphasis on intuition" to foster student understanding. They use the "modern mathematics" method to illustrate their point. Within this approach to teaching mathematics students were first taught to grasp the "basic structure" of mathematics. As students became more familiar with this underlying structure of mathematical functions, they were able to intuitively comprehend higher mathematical operations. As we acquire familiarity with a range of topics, it is not only easier to make connections within one field of knowledge, but these correlations traverse the curriculum. Noddings and Shore (1985, p. 140) recommend this kind of cross pollination and seed planting in all subject areas: "literature may be used effectively in all other subjects to enhance familiarity and invite engagement."

As previously mentioned, Noddings and Shore are primarily interested in promoting student intuition.

There is no discussion of the teachers' use of intuition in their book. The ideas set forth however are as pertinent to teachers' use of intuition as they are to enhancing student intuition. In a discussion I was having with a supervising teacher, the idea of using intuition as the basis of experience was approached. The teacher was making suggestions of what to do with student teachers to improve their teaching proficiency. She associated imagination with intuition in this reference to a particular student teacher: "I really like the idea of asking her to picture what might happen in the classroom, and talk through what she sees as a way to develop imagining. She'll be more comfortable when one of her predictions transpires, or starts out but then goes off on a tangent or whatever. The act of having her picture all that could happen in the classroom will help her practice imagining. Then because she will have had those trial runs, she'll be more comfortable when she's doing the actual teaching and may be freer to go with her intuitions." I frequently ask preservice teachers to picture their ideal classroom. I do this many times throughout a semester course, but usually with variation of purpose and perspective. This imagining again and again is meant to familiarize them with ideas that one day they may put into practice. It certainly can not take the place of real experience, but imagined events can help us feel more comfortable with situations when the future presents itself.

"As with many interwoven threads wrapped around and through the phenomena of teachers' daily use of imagination and intuition, the idea of sensitivity could be a theme discussed by itself" (Jagla 1990, p. 110). We acquire and cultivate our sensitivity to people and circumstances as we become more and more familiar with them. As we gain familiarity with our world through experiences we are constantly perceiving through our senses. The more attuned we are to our senses, the more we are able to reliably use the knowledge gained.

Many feel that intuition is directly correlated to the senses. The more harmonious we are with our own senses, the more intuitive we can be. One teacher said: "I don't think you can be intuitive without being sensitive. I think intuition is the judgment that you make after you have all of the information from your senses . . . Decision-making would not be possible without the sensitivity."

Another teacher agrees that intuition is a heightened sensitivity to incoming information. To him, this sensitivity is more often a deliberate reaction, rather than a spontaneous event: "I don't think it just happens. I think that a lot of times what we call intuition or psychic ability or anything else is really just heightened awareness of the input that's coming in . . . Occasionally things come out of the blue to me as they do for anybody, and I trust that. But usually it is a more studied response. It is also a willingness to say yes to that." Trusting in your own intuition is important.

Do you say yes to the feelings and intuitions that occur in a classroom setting? In what sense does familiarity free you to teach more imaginatively and intuitively?

CHAPTER 6

COMPARE
AND CONTRAST

As we explore the threads of understanding embedded in the fabric of imaginative and intuitive teaching we find strands to compare and contrast. The rich texture of these phenomena provide a tapestry of marvelous dimensions. We can stand back and gaze in awe at its magnificence or we can closely examine the curious splendor of individual threads. As we better recognize the ways these strands match and the ways they vary we can become elegant weavers ourselves, intuitively creating a classroom fabric of imaginative hues.

In this chapter I look at how teachers use their imagination and intuition when working with different subjects or groups. There are similar and disparate methods used with varying classes due to numerous circumstances. Do some subjects lend themselves more or less to the use of imagination and intuition? I consider the themes of resourcefulness, variation and possibilities. These have been alluded to in various ways in previous chapters, here we will focus on them separately. I deliberate imaginative and intuitive teaching with regard to the similarities and differences of randomness versus structure in the classroom. I discuss how teachers feel that imaginative teaching is or is not necessarily linked with intuitive teaching.

Particular Subjects or Groups

This theme is concerned with the manner in which individual curricular subject areas and certain groups of students might affect a teacher's use of imagination and intuition. Many teachers agree that all subjects ought to be taught imaginatively. Imagination and intuition are to be valued and used within all subject domains and with all groups of students. However, the manifestation of these phenomena is sometimes altered from group to group and from one subject area to another. A few teachers have expressed difficulty with the teaching of mathematics, however they all agreed that imaginative teaching is certainly important when attempting to get mathematics concepts across to students. Some teachers felt that math has traditionally been thought of as a "dry subject" because it has been taught that way to many. Too many teachers have typically looked at math as memorization of tables and facts rather than the excitement of problem solving, working out puzzles and answering riddles. To some, this is a dilemma which stems from not having a good understanding of the subject matter before teaching it. To others this is not a good reason. As one teacher put it: "It's a funny thing, sometimes the person who knows their material best, presents it dryly because she sees it all as just matter of fact. And sometimes a person who knows it best can see it as an art. She can get excited about inverse operations in math or whatever." A primary teacher who indicated that mathematics was not always her favorite subject to teach said: "I work a lot harder at the math because I want it to be a positive experience for my second graders. It was not for me. I've belatedly come to understand and appreciate it more now . . . I think it can lend itself to a lot of imaging." An imaginative high school math teacher voiced her opinion: "All subjects lend themselves to imaginative teaching since, to me, they are *all* relatives. Music is omnipotent—the graceful rhythm of the leaves in the wind, the nagging monotony of multiplication tables from the mouths of second graders, the symphony of color, tessellations of Escher, and the frequent thump of your heart when you're isolated in thought." Some teachers felt you could easily present math procedures to students without much use of your imagination, but if you really want the students to apply any of these creative lessons it is necessary to evoke experiential connections.

The use of imagination by a math teacher is essential if her students are to truly grasp the concepts being taught rather than simply memorize facts. Imaginative teachers are able to tap the imaginations of their students so that algebra, geometry, trigonometry, etc., is understood. Imaginative connections to everyday life lend relevance to abstract math concepts. The teacher who teaches geometry by having the students build kaleidoscopes is creatively stretching the students' imaginations and making abstract concepts comprehensible through application. Math and science taught together lend themselves to much imaginative teaching. Einstein's theory of relativity becomes more understandable by following Einstein's own imaginative process with moving trains. Einstein himself thought that "Imagination is more important than knowledge."

A junior high teacher believes that social studies best lends itself to a teacher's use of imagination, although he feels it is essential in all areas: "I think social studies is probably the easiest to use my imagination because I can get the kids involved, by being part of whatever it is. If I'm trying to teach democracy, I can have them become part of the process . . . Social studies lends itself to more creativity." Other teachers feel that the language arts areas might be thought of as more congenial for imaginative teaching. Although some teachers may see themselves as more or less imaginative in certain subjects areas, they all need to be creatively taught. Imagination is not easily quantifiable and the attributes of more and less do not readily apply. Teachers seem to use their imaginations to a greater degree with the areas they enjoy most. Perhaps this is due to a deeper appreciation for the particular subject themselves and the desire to pass this wonder on to their students.

Elementary teachers have the demanding task of teaching all areas of the curriculum. Good elementary teachers know that imaginative lessons stem from creatively planning experiences which integrate the curricular areas to promote involvement, understanding and love of learning. To combine subject areas, teachers necessarily use their imaginations to plan meaningful lessons that involve the students in activities which promote discovery and awareness. If we want our students to make imaginative connections, we as teachers must exercise our own imaginations in teaching them.

Implicitly, intuition is a necessary element of teaching all subject areas as well. The interaction and spontaneity are ever present aspects of effective teaching and learning. Examples of the necessity for facilitating connections and framing contexts for students have been given. This is discussed more extensively in the next chapter. Teachers need to become familiar with their students to be able to "read" them in various subject matter situations, to be able to ascertain the students' interests, to "pick up on" energy levels and to respond, often instantaneously, to given cues. As one high school teacher put it: "I don't teach subjects, I teach students." This statement is perhaps one of the more profound assertions made in this regard.

To keep the individual students foremost in one's mind is the ultimate responsibility of all teachers regardless of subject matter accountability. Unfortunately many high school teachers do not agree with this and tend to concentrate more on their curricular specialty and lose sight of the individual students. It is through this focus on the individuals entrusted to us as students that we as teachers use our intuitions in every day classroom activities. Once again there was much less discussion on teachers' use of intuition regarding different subject areas than their use of imagination because the intuitive responses in teaching relate more directly to the students than to the curricular area being taught.

Regarding different groups of students, an elementary teacher said: "I feel strongly that heterogeneous grouping is healthy. We have so much to learn from one another. It bothers me how much kids are separated and isolated and labeled, because I prefer a mixed group. I think a lot of good things can come from that." She acknowledged, though, that with a group of so called "advanced readers" there is a charged excitement during discussions: ". . . there is a kind of electricity in the air with those advanced readers . . . They really challenge each other . . . they are so creative. That's really an exciting thing to watch." The heterogeneous versus homogeneous grouping debate continues to rage on with no foreseeable conclusive findings. It does appear that we are swinging more toward the heterogeneous mix in elementary schools at this time with the current emphasis on cooperative grouping. It is only in a school with a large enough population that homogeneous groups are possible. Most high schools still "track" students into ability groups, but junior high schools are shifting toward a middle school concept with less emphasis on the homogeneous groups.

I tend to agree with the benefits from a heterogeneous group in a classroom. I go so far as to believe that cross age groups are more beneficial. Of course, this is so antithetical to the current basic structure of most schools that it is difficult to conceive of at present. Teachers in schools where students are clustered into cross-age groups find the process of education to be refreshingly guileless. Frequently in this situation the main method of instruction is individualized with group sharing for projects, demonstrations, etc. Since teachers are more apt to get to know their students on a highly individual basis, they are more inclined to be intuitive when responding to students and making suggestions. Often teachers in schools with traditional grade level groupings will utilize some form of cross age interaction for field trips, special projects, tutoring and after school activities. Teachers need to use their intuition and imagination in any situation they find themselves.

While many teachers feel that they use their imaginations more with a heterogeneous group of students, one teacher insisted that he uses his imagination more while teaching a homogeneous group. Some teachers feel that more creativity is possible with a more advanced group. One teacher believes that it is the remedial students who take to more imaginative lessons rather than the advanced students. But as another teacher points out: "Every child is such an individual so if you have two even in the homogeneous group you have to tune in to each one." This same teacher, however felt that ". . . in the heterogeneous group the range is so much greater that I think you have to be more flexible more creative, so maybe more imaginative in the heterogeneous group." And so the debate goes on. Which makes the most sense to you—heterogeneous or homogeneous groups of students? Does one or the other lend itself more to the use of imagination or intuition?

Some teachers mentioned that sometimes particular groups or individuals will tend to stretch the teacher's imagination more. Certain groups of students might cause a teacher to be more imaginative and sometimes more intuitive no matter if they have been arbitrarily grouped as homogeneous or heterogeneous. As one teacher put it: "The better people in the class are working, the better I will be engaged. It's that we up each other's ante." It seems that all you need is one student who catches your imaginative spark and it is enough to rekindle your own imagination to stretch further. One college teacher told me of a music theory class she was teaching where one of her students was particularly involved with her lectures on Mozart. As she imaginatively brought out the life of the composer, this student's imagination was heightened to the extent that "Mozart was alive in that room." The rest of the class benefited from the lively banter and surely got a much better feel for the attributes of Mozart than they might have through a less imaginative interaction. Using a similar line of thought one could also argue that if a group is not motivated or involved in a lesson, the teacher would need to stretch to use her imagination to a greater degree to challenge the students and inspire them to become involved.

Do certain groups of students require you as a teacher to use your imagination more? Do particular students spark more creative energy in you? Can you be more intuitive when teaching certain subjects? Is your intuition heightened as you get to know your students better?

Resourcefulness

> Seek not, my soul, the life of the immortals; but enjoy to the full the resources that are within thy reach.
>
> —Pythian Odes III, line 109.

An inherent element of the dictionary definition of imagination is the concept of resourcefulness as manifested in the ability to confront and deal with a problem. Being resourceful is being able to use the means at one's disposal to meet situations effectively. A resourceful person is often synonymously referred to as one who is ingenious and inventive. These are adjectives which certainly are not incongruous with imaginative.

Some teachers speak of external resources available to teachers in the form of books and equipment. Other peoples' ideas passed on through writing, conversation, observation, etc., were included as available resources for teachers. Teachers see some link between teachers who are imaginative and teachers who are resourceful. Using available resources is a way of exploring options and possibilities. One teacher was adamant that imagination and resourcefulness were almost one and the same: "That is really the soul of imagination. It's a teacher who can look at a book and see a lesson . . . That's imagination. Whenever you see something, being able to take that and really run with it . . . I got a lot of my imagination out of a book . . . They have a lot of good ideas."

Another teacher does not necessarily equate resourcefulness and imagination, but he views building upon one's resources as a creative endeavor that can be taught: "I've read somewhere something wonderfully creative and I thought, I can do it better than that. I'll remember something that I saw another teacher do and I'll change it to fit my situation. I'll take a simple idea and I'll just keep building on it, building and building on it. So if I have many resources from which to draw, I can change, combine and alter. Good teacher preparation programs and inservice programs should be able to teach resourcefulness."

Conjuring ideas is a way of using your own resources. You imagine varying ways to do something in the classroom to get a concept across to the students, this might include the use of materials, but it is really utilizing your inner resources. The ideas are resources you have stored through reading, watching, discussing or doing. Imaginative planning calls upon this store-house of information. As one teacher said: "You're resourceful in order to think of another way to do it. I don't think of putting the materials out as being resourceful. I won't consciously remember what I did ten years ago and I won't consciously remember what I read in a book, it's going to come."

Veteran teachers all carry with themselves store-houses of resources, both literally and figuratively. Teachers amass loads of ideas as they read about them, try them in their classrooms, or simply hear a colleague's suggestion. These ideas can take the shape of files, notes, reference books, paraphernalia collected for projects or simply notions collected in the archives of the mind. It is often an intuitive insight which will conjure an idea filed in the mind. Once retrieved the imagination takes over to embellish it, to replay in the mind's eye the "video" of how it worked in the past and to preview the perceived reaction of this present group of students. The longer one teaches the more internalized the ideas become and the more teachers' intuitions take over in the daily process of lesson planning and implementation.

Sometimes being resourceful means recognizing a good idea and knowing how to gather the necessary material to implement it. An elementary teacher gave an example of this. During a summer class with students in museology, she was about to embark on a representational project to follow up on a visit to the Museum of Holography. She was beginning to realize that what she had planned would be a little too abstract for the students, when a parent came in to show her what her son had made. It was a kaleidoscope. She realized that the making of a kaleidoscope would be a perfect way to demonstrate what they had learned at the museum, so she rushed around to gather up all of the necessary material: "They made their kaleidoscopes and it was wonderful. I didn't come this morning thinking that was what we were going to be doing, but I was resourceful enough to go with it when it was offered."

The thread of resourcefulness is woven throughout the ideas of both imagination and intuition as they apply to teaching. As teachers spontaneously "come up" with an idea, they are employing some form of intuition for the on-the-spot conjuring of that which is needed. Although often there is much deliberating and imagining used when contemplating possible resources available to teachers, it is sometimes a quick response. The last example where the mother came in with the kaleidoscope that her son had made demonstrates an aspect of the interwoven nature the phenomena of imagination and intuition in teaching. The teacher quickly integrated a resource presented to her and was able to imaginatively adapt her plans to incorporate the idea into the lesson by drawing on material resources available to her in the school. As mentioned, teachers compile a storehouse of resources from which they draw upon at given moments in day-to-day teaching. Some call this an unconscious process, "it's going to come."

Are being resourceful and being imaginative one and the same? What resources do you have available to you as a teacher? How do you utilize these resources imaginatively? Is there any connection between being resourceful and being intuitive?

Variation and Possibilities

> *Variety is the mother of Enjoyment.*
>
> —Benjamin Disraeli in Vivian Grey
> (1826), Book V, chapter 1.

A common thread woven through the idea of using the imagination is being able to picture something in a variety of ways. This was referred to in Part II when defining imagination as looking at all the possibilities. This thread is entwined with the previously discussed theme of "resourcefulness." The teacher utilizes resources to add variety to her manner of presentation. Resources themselves can be considered possibilities. Using the imagination, being creative implies a sense of being innovative or unique. The use of the imagination in teaching presents itself in many ways: devising variations of presentation, designing novel approaches, and generally being innovative. Teachers use their imaginations to create innovative and diverse means to present material to keep students engrossed and involved and to encourage comprehension.

Since teachers must often dwell on the same topic for a substantial amount of time, it is essential to come up with a variety of approaches to keep the students engaged. As one teacher put it: "You need an imagination to get variations of the theme." One teacher referred to variation as an aspect of the art of teaching: "I think sometimes part of the art of teaching is being able to say the same thing in different ways. Whether it be different media or different words. So they can reach the maximum number of people." The current emphasis on differing learning modalities makes the need for variation more obvious. A teacher with a particular learning style must use her imagination to come up with alternative methods of presentation for those students with learning styles different from her own and other members of the class.

Teachers stretch their students' imaginations by having them look at things in a variety of different ways to see other possibilities. A high school history teacher occasionally has his students write a historical event from a new perspective, for example: "Assume for a moment that Germany won the second World War. Write the history of the war, or part of it . . . If you're a Japanese, write the history of the war, assume you've won. Justify Pearl Harbor . . . You begin to see all sides, which to students tends to be very interesting."

One way to stretch your imagination and those of others is to set up boundaries or limits, such as using a specific theme for presentation or relying on a single object as your visual aid. A teacher spoke of imaginative teaching in reference to using a common object to teach various concepts: "You could take an orange. You could teach everything you needed to teach just through an orange." She thinks that being able to conceive of variation is essential to the use of the imagination. If we feel that there is only one proper way to do something we will not deviate to try something new, to imagine how we might do it differently. Much unimaginative teaching stems from this kind of thinking, that there is one correct method. Such unimaginative teaching leads to a lack of interest among the students and consequently a lack of learning and understanding. This is often what happens in classrooms when there is over emphasis on standardized tests, which look for one correct response.

Many school systems base their total evaluation program on these standardized tests given annually. As one teacher put it: "The kind of focus on tests, multiple choice tests, is destroying teaching kids to think for themselves. If you're teaching always to a test, then there's no room for any real learning to occur whatsoever. Because there's only the right answers." Most standardized tests call for one right answer. An imaginative answer which varies from the expected correct response is considered wrong. For example, in a first grade test to measure a child's ability to think sequentially, there are series of pictures in sets of three. The idea is to order the pictures correctly as first, second and last so that a sensible story is depicted. One set of three pictures depict bricks. In one picture there is a fully-built wall, in another picture there is a half-built wall, and then there is a picture of a single brick. Those who wrote the test were assuming a scenario of construction, thus going from the single brick to partial wall to whole wall is the correct answer. Many students indeed guess this to be correct. On the other hand a student who is thinking for himself is going to see that there are more than one answer to how you order those bricks. You can order them any way you want, depending on your explanatory story to accompany the answer.

In a workshop for preservice teachers, the instructor chose to confront these teachers-to-be with the dilemma of the testing emphasis in public schools today. She used the first grade sequencing activity: "Working with university students, most of them pretty bright people, I did that exercise with them. Only I asked them to come up with three separate orderings and to write their rationale for how they got to each one. They thought I was nuts. Most of them did the one thing and said, we've done it. I said, no I want another one. They didn't see why. After all they'd done it and they got it right . . . They were able to see the results and read them aloud. We talked about the difference between all these orderings and the one where you have to get it right. Even then, a lot of them didn't understand. Even though they might have done the exercise and done it well. They still didn't understand why it was necessary to give more than one. That's how deeply ingrained this idea of the one right answer is. So most student teachers are coming into the profession with that kind of indoctrination. That's absolutely appalling." It has been my experience with student teachers and others in undergraduate and graduate education classes that many students are willing to allow for the variation in imaginative answers, however they all understand the reality in the schools, that there will be times when students need to answer some questions differently for the test. It is an interesting dilemma to choose to teach in an imaginative fashion, to get students to think creatively and yet to be evaluated on making sure your students use a much different form of thinking for test taking.

It is heartening to note that many school systems are looking at alternative forms of assessment of student progress. The use of portfolio assessment is in vogue in many school districts to a certain extent. Although sometimes thought of as cumbersome, teachers are becoming increasingly more aware of the necessity of such involved appraisals. All of us as teachers have had students who simply do not test well and those students who are good at guessing and score beyond their normal ability on standardized tests. As we become more cognizant of the need to modify our teaching styles to a variety of student learning modalities, we all become increasingly aware of the necessity for various forms of assessment to accurately demonstrate the progress of our students. Unfortunately the dilemma rests with our societal need for comparison and competition. While it may be obvious to us as teachers that we are best able to formulate assessments of our students based on portfolios and our own daily observation and interaction, it is difficult to accurately compare such results with other teachers across the nation to the satisfaction of the non-teaching segment of the population. Indeed many educators insist on standardized test results for various reasons.

I see no reason to forgo creative teaching in deference to rigid test preparation, however all of us must come to grips with the reality of the tests that our students will encounter. It seems to me that if a student is being educated in an imaginative and creative environment and performing to the best of his/her potential then the test taking issue is secondary. There will be necessary preparation for testing times which will basically consist of review of test taking mechanics. Certainly we cannot let the tests dictate our style of teaching.

Do you think that emphasis on standardized testing inhibits imaginative teaching? How do you resolve the dilemma for yourself?

Randomness versus Structure

> I myself am pursuing the same instinctive course as the veriest human animal you can think of—I am, however young, writing at random—straining at particles of light in the midst of a great darkness
>
> —John Keats from a Letter to George and Georgina Keats (March 19, 1819)

One teacher referred to a more structured use of his imagination as he has gained experience as a teacher: "My imagination, although I still use it, I don't think is as colorful as it used to be when I first started. I think my imagination is much more structured now than it was then." He believes that many of the ideas that he came up with as a beginning teacher were through random occurrences. He attributes this randomness to a lack of inhibition when he was younger. As was noted in the last chapter, many teachers feel they are more imaginative and most definitely believe they are more intuitive as they have gained experience. Do you think you lose some imagination as you get older? If something is structured can it still be imaginative?

Even in an apparently open classroom there is always some underlying structure. A primary teacher compared her current classroom situation with a previous environment when she taught in an alternative school, which shunned the idea of structure: "Nothing is directionless. I'm always providing some structure . . . I used to think that was a bad word and I don't any more. I've had an era of no structure . . . a group of us started an alternative school . . . It lasted for about six years. It was very loose . . . I do think a lot of good things happened naturally. Kids were in a stimulating environment with lots of encouragement from the adults around. They were deeply exploring things of interest to them and they were learning the basic skills in the process. I still believe in that. I used to think structure was a dirty word and now I think it's an important foundation. There can be a great deal of openness and freedom of individual choice and pursuit but there's an underlying structure to it all."

The teacher is conscious of a structure or plan. However during the implementation of that plan, often randomness occurs. Teachers provide a framework by deciding guidelines, time limits, material to be used, format of groups, etc. The teacher consciously chooses the activities or methods to reach the planned goals, but often during the course of a lesson students will be allowed freedom to choose from among the preselected material, decide specifics for activities, and use trial and error methods for tasks at hand. Much of this implementation time will appear random or haphazard to the casual observer.

The interplay of randomness versus structure is an integral part of some teachers' classroom methods. A college teacher included these ideas in her teaching of writing: "If I'm thinking of the teaching of writing for instance, the concepts are: randomness, and then the opposite of randomness which is precision of focus, detail as a sort of vehicle for the attaining of focus. Those are my two main concepts: randomness and focus." During the teaching of a class, I have observed this teacher playing these concepts back and forth. She will ask the students to "focus" on something one minute, often to write down their feelings on a particularly focused idea. Indeed to focus their feelings as they write. The next minute she will have the students do "random drawing" to illustrate other feelings that they might have over-looked.

The randomness allows for the free flow of feeling and insight. Some element of randomness is linked with the idea of intuition and spontaneity. Certainly imaginings are often random in nature. But it appears that often in classrooms there is a necessity to find appropriate structure or focus to expand or enhance the imagination. Indeed the mere process of having students do random drawing is a structure unto itself. As was mentioned in the discussion of "variation," often a structure as a limitation can enhance the imagination. Indeed, artists' creativity often springs from the constrictions and structures that they set up for themselves. For example, a sculptor plans his work by deciding on a subject, the media to be used, an approximate size, etc. The creative process of sculpting is given some focus and direction and it flows from and through the structure. Insight and inspiration may have prompted the design and often subtle intuitive feelings will alter the direction during the process. Some aspects of the process may appear to be random—probably particular actions are indeed random occurrences. But there is still the underlying structure spurring the imagination on.

One teacher links these ideas to the planning and implementation of curricula. The plan being the structure, but in carrying it out in the classroom the teacher is often involved in a random effort. She refers to her plan as her checklist: "My checklist goes like this (shows straight line) and my implementation goes like this (shows random movement). I must have the courage never to know where it's going to go, because that's a matter of trust . . . But I must have my checklist." There may be randomness within the implementation of a planned activity because the teacher does not know where it will lead. However, the structure is often formed through the intuitive insights that guide the direction.

Noddings and Shore (1984, p. 143) advise that taking intuition into account when planning curricula, relates to the manner in which structure ought to be demonstrated to students: "teachers and curriculum makers, who take intuition seriously, will not suppose that presenting a structure ensures that students see a structure . . ." Noddings and Shore indicate that the teacher may be cognizant of the underlying structure of a lesson, but it is necessary to allow the students to realize this structure on their own. The teacher's job, in this instance, is to enhance the student's intuitive mode so that the student is receptive to understand the structure. The teacher, then needs to be able to ascertain what the student has recognized as the structure:

> We do not *present* a structure in such lessons. What we do is to make possible the tracing out of an outline structure by heightening receptivity. This initial presentation, with its complementary receptivity, gives what-is-there a chance to appear. After what-is-there has been received in rich detail, the student must struggle to attach the elements to the appropriate part of the skeleton structure. We still do not assume that the 'student has the structure.' Finally, in the last phase of the lesson, the student is challenged to bring the structure to the foreground while the details fade into the background. (Noddings and Shore 1984, p. 143).

The interplay between structure and randomness appears to be instrumental to intuition at many levels. Useful intuitions do not usually occur except within some sort of structure, however the occurrence of such an insight is seemingly random or at least not part of a logically reasoned structure. Albert Einstein's intuitive mode of understanding often took huge leaps in thinking, but it was typically in reference to some fundamental notion of structure. Referring to his manner of thinking regarding the discovery of some basic principles in physics, Einstein said: "There is no logical way to the discovery of these elemental laws. There is only the way of intuition, which is helped by a feeling for the order lying behind the appearance" (Planck 1933, p. 215).

How do you know when to adapt a lesson? Are you comfortable with improvisation? Is intuition random? Do you allow for random occurrences in your classroom? Is it important to have a balance of structured experiences with happenstance? How do you balance randomness and structure in your classroom situations?

Intuition and Imagination—Necessarily Wedded?

> And Thought leap'd out to wed with Thought
> Ere Thought could wed itself with Speech.
>
> —Alfred Lord Tennyson from
> In Memoriam (1850), 23, stanza 4.

For many teachers imagination and intuition go hand in hand. For some they do not seem to go together. After some reflection on the phenomena of imagination and intuition, one primary teacher now thinks of them in union with each other: "It's hard to conceive of one without the other now. When you first approached me I felt more confident giving you examples of imaginative teaching. I wasn't as sure that I was much of an intuitive teacher. Then the more we talked about it, the more examples I could find of my being both . . . I think my teaching is probably more balanced than I realized."

One high school teacher did not think that imagination and intuition necessarily went together as teacher traits: "Imaginative teachers need not be intuitive. I base the statement on the fact that I've attended lectures that left me almost delirious with ideas yet, at no time did I feel the lecturer was even aware of my presence. It seemed as though we were two separate entities . . . The teacher would have given the same lecture had no one been in the seats. It was superb. But there wasn't anything in what was said that depended on your action or interaction." Thus based on the assumption that one needs to interact with students in order to be intuitive, this teacher shows how someone can use his imagination as a teacher without ever using his intuition. I do not think one necessarily follows the other. I do believe that most of the intuitive understanding which teachers display is indeed manifest during classroom implementation and is often based on some interaction with the students. But even a lecturer to a passive audience might be intuitively altering his presentation on the spot as he feels is appropriate for the moment.

Similarly some teachers say that intuitive teachers are not necessarily imaginative: "They may feel the needs, but may not be creative in meeting them." Another teacher states: "I think that they're complementary, but I don't think that they would necessarily need to go together . . . I've seen people with wonderfully creative ideas miss the boat at the timing and they flop because they were not intuitive enough . . . I know some wonderfully intuitive people who are lacking in imagination."

It has been my experience that good teachers, through genuine care and concern for their students, pick up on cues to guide them to appropriate methods and relevant activities in the classroom. Good teachers make learning meaningful for the students. They provide for experiences which enliven the classroom and bring enjoyment into the learning process. I recognize intuition and imagination as attributes which good teachers possess. Not everyone uses the same terms to describe these characteristics, but nonetheless they are acknowledged by many.

Although neither the word "imagination" nor the word "intuition" is mentioned within the quote presented here, it is relevant while considering the inseparable nature of these traits in good teachers. Rubin (1985, pp. 31-32) uses "creativity" akin to "imagination" and "artistry" with a similar connotation as "intuition:"

> In teaching, creativity and artistry are inseparable. Truly great teachers not only have an instinctive sense about how to work with children, as well as a talent for distinguishing between the significant and the trivial, but they also are able to approach their tasks with fresh vision. Once they have decided upon their objectives, they seek the approach that offers optimum advantage. At this point their creative impulses begin to take hold: they shun the tedious, the mundane, the prosaic, and look for the methods which are novel and appealing. In addition, since no teaching strategy is foolproof, and difficulties can arise in even the most skillfully planned lesson, the creative aspects of artistry are also important in localizing the sources of difficulties and devising shrewd remedies . . . In its simpler forms, inventiveness involves adapting lessons to the needs of each class. In its more complex states, it consists of devising ways to solve instructional problems. Artist teachers routinely *improvise tactics for reaching objectives and overcoming difficulties.* Improvisation is important because modification and adjustments are almost always necessary to improve student learning rate and achievement.

Are you an imaginative teacher? Do you use your intuition frequently in the classroom? What benefit do you see in considering both imaginative and intuitive teaching together?

CHAPTER 7

THE CLASSROOM
COMES ALIVE

What makes some classroom learning circumstances compelling while other school situations are bleak? Why do certain teachers get a reputation for interesting classes while others are labeled boring? I contend that part of the answer lies in how the teachers use their own imaginations and intuition in the classroom. Imaginative lessons bring learning to life for the students—subject matter becomes relevant and meaningful when presented in an imaginative manner. Several themes come to mind regarding such imaginative teaching: interaction, connection-making, putting things in context, storytelling and the emotional issues of an exciting classroom with an imaginative and intuitive teacher who is loving and caring. These topics have been touched on in previous chapters. This chapter examines the texture of these threads in greater detail.

Is it imaginative to promote interaction in your classroom? How do you use your imagination to help students make connections with concepts and place these ideas into a framework or context? Are good teachers necessarily storytellers? What does emotion have to do with the school environment? In what ways do you show love and care in the classroom?

Interaction

The theme of interaction is important and inherent to intuitive and imaginative processes in classrooms. For the imaginative and intuitive teacher there needs to be interaction with oneself, with and among the students, with colleagues, with the subject matter and with the context.

Teachers need to interact with the students in the class. One teacher referred to an "interactive truth" in the classroom where the class becomes a part of the imaginative process. Thinking interactively is not necessarily deliberate or conscious. Teachers are constantly negotiating with their students as a meaning-making process. The teacher's action at these times is designed in the moment. This type of action both utilizes and provides practical knowledge. The teacher is both designing and reflecting in action. This is an interactive process. Schon (1983) states that teachers carry on a "reflective conversation" with the immediate situation at hand. Schubert (1975) refers to this process as situational analysis. Schubert (1986) elaborates on various interactions between and among Schwab's (1971) four commonplaces: teacher, learner, subject matter and milieu. Elbaz (1983) says that practical knowledge is formed in situations as a response to the encounter.

As was mentioned in chapter 4, one teacher's entire view of teaching is a continual conversation with the students, to her there is no teaching unless there is interaction. Greene and Weade (1988, p. 1) similarly regard "teaching-learning processes as conversational processes through which teachers and students collectively construct meaning." This communicative interaction is the basis of education.

The teacher sets the tone in the classroom for meaningful interaction to occur. There must be a positive feeling in a class for worthwhile interaction to transpire.

One teacher laid out the bottom line: "If the atmosphere isn't positive and you're having the true sorrows of a beginning teacher, there's no imagination and intuition, there's survival. So, first of all, the interaction has to be civil. There has to be civility in the classroom and among the people in order for imagination and intuition to be allowed to be there among the teacher and the children." Not all beginning teachers experience "true sorrows," but certainly many of us have experienced classrooms where bickering and sometimes actual fighting are the type of interaction you see among students. Unfortunately this is occasionally fostered by a teacher's negative attitude regarding basic control and discipline. So although "civility" might sound like a minimal requirement it can be difficult to achieve in some instances. Ideally you would like to see all students caring about each other, at least to be careful of each other's feelings. You may have students who really do not like each other for one reason or another, so you may not be able to insist that they be nice to each other but surely you can insist that they be civil. Usually in a positive classroom environment the deeper kind of caring emerges.

Many teachers firmly believe that there is no teaching occurring if there is no interaction. One teacher reminds us that quality interaction need not involve speech: "It is possible to simply present material without interaction, but that's not teaching. It doesn't always need to be a verbal interaction. A lecture can be interactive. Television shows arc interactive." Clearly interaction can take on varying connotations. The teacher interacts with the students and facilitates students' interaction among each other. A good teacher will also promote student interaction with the subject matter, ideas, objects or relevant material. One way teachers foster such interaction is through valuing all the ways students are able to interact with the material presented.

The need to be able to see the students' faces in order to "read" them for feedback to see "whether you're getting through or not" is how one teacher uses interaction in the class. Of course, besides the non verbal interaction, direct discussion and divergent questioning allow teachers to understand what their students are thinking. Interaction is a key factor to relevant teaching and learning.

Unfortunately, meaningful interaction is not as prevalent as one might think. A high school teacher acknowledged the fact that many, in fact most, of the teachers in her school do not teach in an interactive manner. The tendency is to dole out the work to the students and to sit down while they do it: "But this is going to be the death of education, all these cockamamy textbooks with the ditto masters."

Many good teachers voice the position that the ability to relate to students is more important than knowledge of subject matter. One teacher said: "If I were principal of a school and I had the choice of hiring a person who was knowledgeable in his subject field but could not relate or someone who could relate to people but was not knowledgeable, which would I choose? The one who could relate . . . if you can get them to the point where they know learning is fun, it pays off." Motivation is paramount. You must interact with the students in order to encourage them to want to learn in the first place. Once they are interested, interaction with teacher, peers and subject matter broadens understanding.

A second grade teacher, who runs a highly interactive second grade classroom, feels that the children have so much to learn from each other: "It's important to emphasize interaction among the children. They need to talk so they can learn from one another, see ways other people think, imagine them, respond to them intuitively . . . There's so much variety in how people approach things. Talking out loud helps you decide how much you've learned and what meaning it has for you. The kids need to do that. That should be encouraged." Indeed, such lively discussion is encouraged at all levels in classrooms where teachers know the value of interaction. Such interaction promotes improved functioning of students' imaginations and enhanced understanding of the subject matter at hand. It does not matter whether we are talking about second graders or sophomores, it is important that teachers provide for student interaction. Sharing the experience is an important aspect to more profound understanding.

It is important to remember the quieter students when declaring the necessity of peer interaction. Some teachers attempt to get the reticent learners to become more verbal. This just may not be in their personality. As the teacher one must become more conscious of different ways that people can communicate other than verbally. Certainly it is more difficult to assess the quality of interaction of the less verbal student, but it does not mean that this type of learner cannot be encouraged to interact in other ways. It is important to note that because a student is not particularly verbal does not necessarily mean that he is not imaginative or intelligent. Albert Einstein did not speak until the age of three and had much difficulty with speech for many years after that. He was a solitary individual, often intensely involved in his own imaginings, but not always sharing these with others. Teachers need to be sensitive to the various ways that children interact with others and with themselves.

Compelling students to love learning is what gets them involved. Full participation, on the part of the student, is necessary for learning to take place. Motivating students to get them interacting with the daily assignments and activities in the classroom is a significant aspect of good teaching. It is so important that students be actively engaged in whatever is going on in the class, instead of just passively sitting there taking it in. They need to be active explorers with the teacher facilitating discussions, wondering aloud, and making connections. As one teacher put it: "Most of it involves hooking their imaginations, letting them think and create."

Encouraging students to write is an example of promoting meaningful interaction. But there is nothing more intimidating for many students than to be given a blank sheet of paper and be told to go write a story. Most respond: "I don't know what to write." Pre-writing activities such as brainstorming and creative discussion get students actively engaged in the learning process. As one high school English teacher stated: "The more engaged they are in their learning the more they are going to enjoy it. The more they enjoy it the more they are going to learn. It's obvious and yet difficult to accomplish."

There is a strong bond between interaction and fun or enjoyment in learning. Classrooms where students are highly engaged in the learning process through interaction with their teacher, each other, the ideas and material, are places where excitement and enjoyment are evident. Student imaginations are obviously engaged when the students are excitedly involved in projects and discussions in the classroom. It takes imaginative planning on the part of the teacher to instigate these activities and provide a supportive environment. It takes an intuitive teacher to continually adjust and readjust details and facilitate particular interactions throughout such stimulating lessons.

In any given class there will be students at varying levels of engagement all the way from those who might be actively assisting in "teaching" the class to those who might be irritated with the involvement process and wish the teacher would just get on with imparting information for the test. A college teacher said that as long as she got one person in the class involved and interested, typically the spark would spread: "The higher the caliber of engagement, then the better a thing will be going on. It only takes one other person who is enormously, excitedly engaged . . . What it's our job to do, teachers and students together, is to work together to get the spark . . . When there isn't a spark we've departed from an interactive notion of learning to a me knowing and they don't . . . if it's not interactive then nothing's happening."

It is the interaction that helps to bring learning to life. Here the themes of "interaction" and "connection" overlap. Making connections is an interactive process, but the person-to-person interaction in a class is a type of connection-making in and of itself. In chapter 4 I mentioned an example from a music history course on the college level. Because of the teacher's involvement into who Mozart was, her own excitement and active imagination brought the man to life in the classroom. She tells us: "I really led the class into who Mozart was, because I love Mozart so much. Everything that I'm saying was new and Mozart was just alive in the room in my mind. Because he was alive in my mind—all human truth is interactive—and he was alive in the minds of those who were with me."

This teacher elaborated on the idea of "interactive truth": "My truth is an interactive truth, it's out here that it happens—between us. Einstein brought a new truth into the twentieth century, Einstein amongst others. Interaction is the enormous mystery. It isn't that I'm dealing only with one or two. It's that through this interaction with however many specific students it happens to be, Mozart is alive in the class, period, for anybody who wishes to participate in it." Interaction is slightly different from the college level to the elementary classroom, yet it is quite similar in most respects. At all levels imaginative and intuitive teachers are attempting to excite and engage their students for the purpose of understanding and enjoyment in learning.

Interaction within the class and with the subject matter is one thing that makes the material alive and meaningful for the learners. It is in making things come alive and keeping them alive in the classroom that teachers are continually using their own imaginative and intuitive capacities. A teacher's vivid image of an historical event, a mathematical algorithm or a poem is what is keeping that entity alive for the teacher, who in turn imparts this living excitement to the students. As the students become excited with the living presence of a particular idea, the energy increases as the interaction moves back and forth. It is this process that makes something relevant and interesting for the students and therefore more readily comprehendible. This type of imaginative encounter requires continuous intuitive capabilities on the part of the teacher. The teacher reads and spontaneously interprets students' energy levels and particular interests and is thereby able to capitalize on momentary connections for individuals as well as for the whole group. It is probably through some intuitive understanding that the teacher has decided to use a particular tact to bring something to life. It is certainly intuition that enables the teacher to help sustain the life for an appropriate period. This process of "bringing things to life" can be called putting things "in context" for students.

How do you use your imagination when you interact with your students? with the classroom environment? with the content? with yourself? In what ways does you intuition come into play during these times of interaction?

Connections and Context

> Each time new resonances are awakened, new connections disclosed, I am made aware of the uses of imagination and its place in helping me penetrate the "world."
>
> —Maxine Greene (1988, p. 54)

The thread of interaction is entwined with the notion of making connection and putting things in context for students. If a teacher is facilitating the making of connections through relevant questions, comments and activities, she is obviously interacting with the students. As students make their own connections by placing ideas in context they are interacting with the material. However, connection and context, as themes to ponder separately from the idea of interaction, are significant.

Connection making and contextual understanding are inherent in some teachers' definitions of imagination. A teacher said: "Part of the imagination is a sense of things always in context . . ." She has pointed out that the "fullness" of things, looking at "wholes" instead of "disassociated parts," putting things into context for students, are all powerful facets of imaginative teaching. In order to promote understanding for our students we need to convey "imaginative fullness." In order to provide context for a topic we need to illustrate connections with the past, present and future. Making relevant connections and formulating appropriate context is what makes sense of subject matter for students. Not only must there be connection within the content, but there also should be a connection between the teacher and the student, among the students and among teachers in a school community.

Although they use the word "image," Connelly and Clandinin (1985, p. 198) paint a comparable picture of connection in time:

> Image is here conceptualized as a kind of knowledge embodied in a person and connected with the individual's past present and future. Image draws both the past and the future into a personally meaningful nexus of experience focused on the immediate situation that called it forth. It reaches into the past gathering up experiential threads meaningfully connected to the present. And it reaches intentionally into the future and

creates new meaningfully connected threads as situations are experienced and new situations anticipated from the perspective of the image. Image emerges from the imaginative processes by which meaningful and useful patterns are generated in minded practice.

While observing her teaching a college course on Aristotle I witnessed a teacher's connection-making in action. The associations were sometimes initiated by the teacher and sometimes by students. The teacher told me: "I see my job in teaching Aristotle as making my own connections, helping them to make theirs. When they're talking about something else, I will often make a connection to something else in Aristotle . . . Then we get out the books. Or somebody else remembers something else. We're going back and forth between our own immediate experience, our own memory and the text at hand. Aristotle is always being kept alive now. Because so long as he's back there and there's not our sense of history being awakened, then we're not going to have much interest in Aristotle."

In the teaching of anything historical it is important to always connect with the students' present lives or they will often become weary of the content and thus less engaged for comprehension. Connection to our own lives is what makes anything relevant. It is the making of these connections and the finding of the appropriate context that makes learning "come alive" and be meaningful and relevant. Without the relevancy the significance is missing.

An administrator of an arts-in-education organization told me a story which involved an artist-in-residence she was supervising in an elementary school writing project. This artist was working with a sixth grade class, during the time the sixth graders were studying ancient Greece. The students were doing some research on the topic. The artist asked the students about their images concerning ancient Greece. Even though their teacher had been "teaching" them about the subject for some time, there were many misconceptions: "There were some kids who thought that Greek people now walked around in Togas. There were other kids who thought that they drove cars in ancient Greece . . . The teacher . . . didn't know about these misconceptions because she had been teaching out here as only out here. You learn these facts about ancient Greece. It doesn't matter about your connection. You learn these facts. You go out and you do research and you bring back what you've done and you copy from the dictionary or from the encyclopedia or whatever. What's left out there, is there's no imaginative connection between the kid and the subject matter." The context was lacking for the majority of those students. The teacher seemed to be imparting factual knowledge and thought she was involving the students by having them "research" their own facts. But what was missing was the connection in the minds of the students. Often questioning rather than telling engages students to think and make sense of the subject matter at hand. Encouraging students to ask their own questions will make examples relevant and research more meaningful.

Teachers need to utilize their imaginations in planning activities and lessons which promote connection making and provide relevant context for the students. While planning, a teacher can predict certain possible connections and individualize them for particular students in the class. When looking back at the day's lessons, a teacher can also come up with more connections after deliberating and evaluating how well information was received by the students. It is the teacher's responsibility to assist the students with such reinforcement of what they have experienced so that it is absorbed and understood. Since teachers are constantly evaluating and reflecting spontaneously throughout classroom activities and lessons, some of these connections are interjected by the teacher through her intuitive responses. In addition, the student's own intuition regarding himself and the information being presented generates pertinent connections and makes the context "come alive."

Many good elementary teachers strongly feel that the best way to teach is by connecting subject areas so that they are not studied in isolation from one another. A current trend in education at this level is interrelating subject matter. The traditional approach to the teaching of language has been one of isolation of skills—reading, writing, spelling, handwriting have all been taught as separate subjects. Unfortunately this has led to monotony and disinterest on the part of many students. Thankfully, school districts are picking up on current research which urges the connection of these obviously related areas. The "imaginative fullness" is returning to the instruction of language arts. The teaching of reading and writing is connected to other subject areas, thus increasing understanding and excitement and helping students make sense of the curriculum.

A particularly gifted primary teacher who has been teaching more than twenty-five years has always made these connections even though it was not popular for a period of time: "If activities in the classroom can be natural, like real life, they are more effective. I resent having to segment the day. It's always so exciting when everything comes together. Somebody walking in wouldn't know exactly what it is we're doing because I integrate the curriculum as much as possible." This teacher feels that making connections obvious for students and assisting them to formulate a context is an imaginative process: "To be imaginative enough to put concepts in terms that will make connections for kids so they'll take off in their own minds is a real gift. We learn best what we can relate to. Things put into the context of our lives and what's important to us help us to see the whole rather than isolated parts."

Another fourth grade teacher who has been teaching more than thirty years similarly feels that the idea of helping students make connections and discern relevant contexts is a significant aspect of teaching. She acknowledges that this is often a difficult task as a teacher: "Figuring out what the context is for the kids, that's an important thing to do and it's not easy . . . to put it into their experience so they can understand it." It takes the imaginative capabilities of the teacher to think as the students and come up with the appropriate activities and experiences which will enable them to perceive the context and connect to the issues at hand.

The fourth grade teacher says that sometimes making the connection for students means giving them the "around words" they need to make sense. Sometimes students are puzzled by particular words or phrases used to explain something. Further interpretation using other words to illustrate the point is warranted. So often when students do not understand something a teacher will simply reiterate what was said until the student gives up and carries on the best as he can. Asking a student just what it is he does not understand will usually frustrate him further. If he knew that he could probably figure the rest out for himself anyway. Instead figuring out the misconception or lack of understanding together helps give the student a model for problem solving and makes the teacher more sensitive to that student's needs. As one teacher put it: "Sometimes you just want to see where they're coming from." Teachers need to determine students own contextual frameworks to be able to assist each individual in the class. One student may be "coming from" a different contextual base than another.

One high school teacher thinks that a comprehensive understanding of the subject matter involved provides the teacher with the capability to facilitate these connections for students: "If you have something to hang a topic on, and you put it in a place in your lesson that would be receptive to the students. That comes from knowledge of subject. If a person is able to make liaisons within his major field as well as among others, then this person has the tools for imaginative presentation." It is not an easy task—you need to know your subject matter well and you need to know the students in order to prompt connections and provide a meaningful context. Good teachers use their imaginations to plan relevant experiential activities because often concrete experience affords students a relevant context for ideas and promotes the making of connections.

In order to "make it come alive" for the students so that the students can make their own connections, teachers offer stories and dramatizations as a means to provide the students with a meaningful context. One high school teacher I spoke with makes connections from history to the present day lives of his students. He is able to facilitate this connection making through the thorough understanding he has of his students and his empathy with high school age students by remembering what it was like to be in high school, himself. He is a sympathetic, approachable and accessible person who has established a warm, open environment in his classes. Therefore, his students feel comfortable enough to explore their own imaginative connections to topics. This non-threatening atmosphere he has created encourages the students to question, experiment and explore. This allows them to discover their own meaningful connections and contexts. Since students are not afraid to speak out, challenge ideas or bring up an issue important to them, they are able to clarify ideas which helps them make meaningful connections. This teacher uses role playing and simulations to create a context which helps elucidate many concepts. In one of the classes that

I observed, the students had just completed video tapes which they had worked on in small groups. This was in a sophomore communication arts class. It was not only meant as a creative experience, but was mainly a lesson in group dynamics. The process put many skills together for the students in a meaningful context.

Sometimes it is necessary to create a new context for particular students based on their interest. This teacher is sensitive to the interests of his students: "When the occasion arises I will change an assignment for one particular student in the class. I was teaching an English class a couple of years ago. I had this one girl who was a wonderful writer. I kept getting more and more frustrated because she was getting so bored in class." He suggested that she write her own book and not attend his class any more. As you might imagine the girl was dumbfounded. He explained that they would meet during the lunch hour and he would assist her with the project. The girl used the class period to do her writing in the word processing lab. That teacher's imagination and intuition came together to help create an alternative learning situation for a student who really needed this opportunity: "At the end of the year she had completed the first hundred pages. It was very good. It was *really* good. She is now at Northwestern (University) on a writing scholarship."

Making connections gives rise to intuitive comprehension. For example, by making a spontaneous connection from a previous experience to a situation you find yourself immersed in at present can provide you with a valuable insight. Another example of intuitive connection-making might be to momentarily reflect on a student's reaction as it is occurring and spontaneously link that to an appropriate response which you imagined during your lesson planning. The teacher's use of intuition is apparent in the above scenario involving the creation of a new context for the girl who was bored in the standard English class. As was mentioned at the end of the section on interaction, intuitive connections are made by teachers to keep subject matter alive.

In what ways do you utilize your intuition when you assist a student in making a relevant connection to the subject matter at hand? What imaginative methods have you come up with to provide contextual understanding for your students? Do you think that you use your intuition more when you help students make connections and your imagination more when your provide a context?

Storytelling

> *The narrator must seek to imbue himself with the life and spirit of the time . . . He must, himself be, as it were, a sharer or a spectator of the action he describes.*
>
> —Francis Parkman, from
> Pioneers of France in the
> New World (1865), introduction.

Some of the thematic threads I have been attempting to unravel are more delicately woven than others. The thread of interaction is intricately woven with the thread of connection making, it is difficult to discuss one without the other. So, too, the theme of storytelling weaves in, around and through many other thematic threads. When telling a story a teacher interacts with her class in order to facilitate imaginative connections by describing a context which "makes things come alive" for the students.

Storytelling is a delightfully imaginative activity for all ages. Often people outside the field of education think of storytelling as an endeavor for kindergarten and maybe primary grades. But the telling of stories is a wonderful way to provide context and make connections for students at any level. The more engaged the storyteller is the more involved the listeners will be—it can be an interactive process where the students experience the story as an event. A high school teacher told me he often uses storytelling to involve the students: "Sometimes my use of imagination will come in telling stories to the class and letting them try to experience what history was like."

Stories fascinate students and through the teacher's use of his own imagination these stories can "come alive." Often it is the teacher's use of intuition which guides him through a story and helps him decide when to pause and ask pertinent questions or to encourage students to react or respond in ways which will promote connection making. It is his intuition which leads the teacher to select storytelling as the method of presenting a lesson at appropriate times and steers him toward another technique for other lessons.

A primary teacher who is also a professional story-teller uses this technique in her second grade classroom as a means of encouraging the students' own imagina-tions and prompting connection making: "If I can relate a little anecdote to help them make an association it is helpful. We create lots of story problems in the room about ourselves to reinforce mathematical concepts. We take it from the abstract to the personal and concrete." Storytelling can be anecdotal or more structured depend-ing on the situation.

There is a sort of "magic" in the air in any class-room when an imaginative teacher is telling a story to her class. When she is in the midst of this magical sto-rytelling process, the second grade teacher, mentioned in the preceding paragraph, uses her intuition to gauge the level of involvement of the students: "I think that story-telling is a marvelous teaching tool . . . The language just draws you into the experience. I see such a differ-ence between reading to children—and I think there are some wonderful books to read aloud to them—but there's such a magic about telling a story. We're all going through this together and there's immediate rapport. I know what they're seeing in their minds' eye by the looks on their faces . . . I think the expressions on their faces are really revealing as is general body language . . . as they get drawn into the story, they're transported . . . I'm taking them there . . . It just happens. They . . . give themselves over to it." This is indeed a powerful teaching technique well worth mastering.

Storytelling in the classroom is an imaginative teaching tool. Its application to language arts and social studies is readily apparent, but it is a useful method to employ in all areas of the curriculum. Storytelling in the classroom often takes the form of relating anecdotes which help to provide a context for the topic at hand. It is significant to note that telling stories and anecdotes usually makes learning a much more enjoyable experience for all involved. When students are engaged and amused they are more likely to comprehend what is being presented and more apt to retain the information for future use: "The great enjoyment that children take in storytelling cannot be overemphasized. Extremely effective teachers often will find that they can communicate about a subject very well if they can bring in an actual personal narrative or tell an incident about a relative or friend that bears on the content of the didactic material" (Singer 1973, p. 247). Here we see the thematic threads of "storytelling" and "interaction" entwined.

Kieran Egan (1986) inquires into the use of storytelling as a valuable teaching technique. He views the school curriculum as the great stories our culture has to offer and the teachers as our culture's storytellers. In his comprehensive book, *Teaching as Storytelling: An Alternative Approach to Teaching in the Elementary School,* he proposes that teachers create lessons by using aspects of the story form. He suggests that we substitute the idea of "story" for what we usually consider the content we need to teach. Egan contends that when we view content as a story to be told we generate the emotional significance of the content. The teacher determines how to provide the connections to this emotional quality and how to relate it in a lucid fashion for the students. Egan indicates that this method does not neglect the facts, but rather emphasizes the development of these facts so that student comprehension is enhanced.

Telling a story from memory, rather than reading it out loud to a class is a more powerful use of the teacher's imagination. Egan correlates the memory and imagination: "One might almost say that the imagination was born from the need to remember" (Egan 1988b, p. 4). If you are telling a story rather than reading aloud to students you are not only engaging your own imagination more, you are further involving the students with you. You are more free to respond intuitively to the individuals in the class because you are relating directly to them without a paper or book between you: "Within the story, the narrator can engage the affective response of the hearers to whichever elements they wish" (Egan 1988b, p. 6). He thinks that storytelling enhances the meaning in a lesson by surrounding the content "with the qualities that engage the imagination in the process of learning."

I taught a staff development workshop course for teachers which I called "Storytelling, Guided Imagery and Other Imaginative Journeys." Some teachers who participated in the class were reticent about their abilities as storytellers. We talked about the use of anecdotes. Most teachers tend to utilize anecdotes to add relevance to subjects or place things in context, sometimes without even realizing the process. By practicing with our own anecdotes and eventually moving into more planned renditions of stories, even the most inhibited teachers can master the art. Giving the students a part in the telling process can often take some of the onus off a hesitant storyteller. Usually, once the students become involved the imagination takes over and storyteller and listener feed off of each other's visions. Any subject is enhanced through this technique. One of the participants in the class was a gym teacher who told wonderful stories and guided the students through imagined games before they actually got to play. This improved their understanding of the game and lessened the likelihood of injury.

Guided imagery is somewhat a derivative of the storytelling technique. Typically in the guided imagery process the students are asked to close their eyes and are led through brief relaxation exercises. The teacher then leads the students through a planned scenario stopping often to allow the students to respond in their own imaginations. For example if you are leading the students through a sunny field you might ask them to stop and smell, touch, gaze at certain things or just at what they conjure for themselves. It is different from storytelling in that less details are given by the teacher. It is a marvelous technique to use for a pre-writing activity or anytime you would like to engage students individual imaginations in a calm manner. It is essential to process the experiences after a guided imagery experience. Sharing their images with the whole class or in small groups helps enrich the entire procedure.

If at anytime you feel something is just not making sense to the students you need only to gather them around and explain it in story form. "The missing link that can bring learning and imagination together to ensure more meaningful learning . . . is the story" (Egan 1988b, p. 8).

Do you tell stories in your classroom? Do you think this is an important skill to master? Do you engage the students to become storytellers also?

Emotion—Excitement, Love and Caring

> Imagination may be called the reflection of the
> emotional life.
>
> —Ruth Griffiths (1935, p. 187)

One cannot discuss imagination without discussing emotion. Excitement fills the air in a classroom when the imagination is aroused. Through the discussion of making connections I showed how excitement is generated as students make their own imaginative correlations. When we make lessons "come alive," through building a relevant context, by storytelling, dramatization, role playing, or other imaginative methods, we are creating excitement in the classroom. In oral cultures as storytellers handed down tradition, their characters, events and situations were brought to life "because they created powerful images. These were not simply imagined events or characters charged with binding ties of emotional attachment. These techniques stimulated—in a sense brought into being—the imagination, that ability to be moved by, to behave as though one perceives and is affected by, what is actually not present or real" (Egan 1988a, p. 117).

Referring to when an imaginative connection is made by a student a fourth grade teacher told me: "It's exciting and real and alive. The excitement of learning something new and how wonderful how all these pieces fit together and it makes sense. There's an order to it. Those are the things that are exciting." The excitement is addictive and it spreads throughout a class. The excitement is often inherent in the subject matter itself and is manifested in the students. This electricity created by imaginative connection and understanding surges as it sweeps through the classroom environment.

A couple of teachers referred to the imaginative excitement of the classroom as a "drug" or something addictive which made them want to produce such lessons over and over again. An elementary teacher said: "That excitement, maybe that's the drug, that makes me want to be imaginative, because you want to get that high and do it again. It keeps you going." A high school teacher has a similar feeling from using her imagination in the classroom: "It's just a free flowing thing. I have never done drugs. But I've had people discuss to me the effects that they give. And that's probably one, like being on kind of an educational high. Imagining and using your imagination in class. Or anywhere else for that matter." Other teachers relayed similar reactions to moments in the classroom when imagination is at a peak. A junior high teacher said: "The times when I have felt most imaginative, I have felt incredibly emotionally charged. Sometimes even to the point where you want to cry. It's like winning an athletic event. You just feel charged."

Intuition is also an emotional issue. It is an inherent part of the idea of making connections and bringing subject matter to life in classrooms and in the minds of the students. A teacher's use of intuition enables her to use her imagination to spark excitement in the classroom. When we have an intuitive insight we often refer to it as a "feeling." Intuition stirs up feelings and emotions. An intuitive teacher is also a loving and caring person who is in touch with her own feelings and those of the students.

Good teachers, in general, exhibit genuine care and concern for their students. Something that is noticeable from going into their classrooms is the way they really listen to their students and dialogue with the students in a sharing and caring manner. Noddings (1984) views teachers who intently listen to their students and involve themselves in sincere discussion with the students as caring people. She sees the "talking and listening, sharing and responding to each other . . . (as) vital in every aspect of education" (Noddings 1984, p. 186). Teachers gain the familiarity needed for intuitive reactions by carefully listening to their students. One teacher told me about the fundamental message she grasped from her courses with Bruno Bettleheim at the University of Chicago: "Listen to children, they have something to tell you." Of course a caring, concerned teacher "listens" to much more than students' words.

There are other commonalties noticeable in the classrooms of quality teachers. One of these is the excitement and energy level that can be felt. Students are actively engrossed in activities that they enjoy. This enjoyment stems from another mutually shared attribute of good teachers. They all love teaching. The teacher's enjoyment inspires the students' delight in and love of learning. As one teacher put it: "The single most important factor in any classroom is the teachers' feeling about what they are doing. My students know that I genuinely enjoy what I'm doing. My classes really respond to that. They have fun. They enjoy it. They know that I'm there because I want to be there. I'm passionate about teaching. I love what I do." Noddings and Shore (1984, p. 168) believe that love of teaching and learning is critical to all of education: "there is the love of teaching and learning, a love that is at the center of the entire educational enterprise. Without a love of teaching in the broadest sense, teachers can do little that is useful . . ."

Good teachers continue to love to learn as much as they love to teach. Love of learning and love of teaching "go hand in hand." As one teacher notes: "There is something in common with loving to learn. Most teachers that I have ever met who are good teachers, do enjoy learning themselves. You could be a professional student. It's a difference between somebody being stagnant as opposed to alive and alert." Exemplary teachers continually take more courses, attend workshops and are vociferous readers. This love of learning manifests itself in various ways, not all take more education courses or workshops in their particular subject area or related to teaching. Many develop avocations in other fields and often share their new learning with enthusiasm in their classes. In all cases there is a burning desire to keep learning and discovering. It would be difficult to instill a love of learning in your students if you did not passionately feel this yourself.

One teacher told me that she feels it is essential to promote the idea of love of learning to student teachers, and to advocate the liberal arts notion of love of subject matter: "It used to be that people taught stuff that they loved. There weren't education departments which taught people how to teach things. When we educate students to teach, it's our job to make them love learning. They need to be able to love learning while they're being students. The young teacher's heart and soul really needs to be in the knowing of the things and the loving of the communicating of the things. All the teachers I ever had who really taught me, were people who loved what they were teaching and then also loved sharing it with somebody else."

A teacher's love of subject matter is significant. Students know whether a teacher enjoys what he is teaching or not. When a teacher truly loves the field that he is teaching, his enthusiasm and excitement are apparent and students are immediately captivated and involved with the subject. Noddings and Shore (1984, p. 166) agree that "love of subject, (is) something that either students or teachers can feel." They believe that teachers' use of intuition is an essential element which helps to convey this fervor for a particular subject to their students. Obviously, students' subtle intuitions are an important element as well:

> In order for this communication to happen, several things must be present: a fascination with the particular subject, an intuitive sense of some (but not necessarily all) of its relationships and concepts, a desire to give this knowledge to others, and the ability to communicate effectively and engagingly. Intuition figures importantly in each of these factors, for the teacher needs to draw upon instantaneous impressions of stu-

dents' interests and aptitudes, the atmosphere of the classroom on any given day, and many other factors that cannot be analyzed rationally in the fluid, dynamic setting of the schoolroom. Intuition needs to be cultivated and trusted as the teacher decides how, when, and in what amount information about the subject should be communicated. But we must keep in mind that not only factual information but *love* of the subject area can be communicated, and for the latter we have no simple procedures, no foolproof strategies. The most specific statement we can make is that a caring teacher who is genuinely excited about a subject or approach will convey this excitement to some of the students . . . (Noddings and Shore 1984, p. 168).

Love is a vital aspect of good teaching. Quality teachers display love and concern for their students, their subject matter, and for teaching and learning in general. One high school teacher's definition of imagination includes the idea of love: "Imagination is letting your love be translated into your classroom . . . So I see imagination as being a passionate activity, because it is a loving thing to do." This same teacher echoes Noddings and Shore's notion of the need for genuine care on the part of the teacher. He had used the word "care" in both his definition of imagination and that of intuition. Once, when trying to clarify his definitions I asked him if what he was saying is that imagination means caring fervently about your subject matter, and intuition is caring about your students. He agreed that it was "something along that line." But that "really caring, though, is the bottom line to it. It's the common silk that weaves through the whole experience of teaching."

I tell you there is no such thing as creative hate!

—from The Song of the Lark (1915), part I

PART IV

PURSUING
THE ELUSIVE IMAGE

I hope the attempts to clarify teachers' use of imagination and intuition in their daily activities, through definitions, metaphors, examples, and discussion have given you a clearer perception of these phenomena.

This final part of the book does not propose to draw any artificial conclusions, but rather to continue the ongoing appreciation of insights to be gleaned from such reflection. This book merely enters into a timeless conversation here and is meant to pose more questions than it answers. By offering some interpretation of the everyday marvels and miracles manifested by imaginative and intuitive teachers, I mean to spark further inquiry and reflection.

Here, I examine ways to encourage teachers to use their imaginative and intuitive capabilities, suggestions for enhancing intuition and imagination in students and, in a final chapter, I offer some further inferences and directions.

What are some concerns you have about using your imagination or intuition in the classroom? Is it necessary that all teachers be imaginative or intuitive?

CHAPTER 8

CULTIVATING
TEACHERS' USE
OF IMAGINATION
AND INTUITION

A Sensitive Plant in a garden grew,
And the young winds fed it with silver dew,
And it opened its fan-like leaves to the light . . .

—Percy Bysshe Shelley from
The Sensitive Plant (1820),
part I, stanza 1

Many teachers value the use of imagination and intuition in daily classroom activities. We equate good teaching with the implementation of these modes. Examination of ways to foster teachers' use of imagination and intuition is significant to the advancement of exemplary education. We need to encourage ourselves and each other to be open to explore areas such as imagination and intuition as they relate to our daily teaching strategies. By being supportive of such endeavors, we strengthen our abilities to truly inspire the generation of youngsters entrusted to us.

Is it important to encourage teachers' use of imagination and intuition? Is it possible to teach this to teachers or to teacher candidates in college course work? How can we promote the use of teachers' imaginations and intuition?

Promoting the Use of Imagination with Teachers

As I talked with teachers regarding the encouragement of imaginative teaching, all were quick to agree with the necessity for such support, but often hesitant as to how this should occur. Can you teach someone to be imaginative? One high school math teacher felt that imagination was a trait that could not be taught: "There are some people who just come to the classroom, they come to life with imagination . . . Maybe some people's sensitivity to set off the imagination is greater than others . . . I think that some people may just not have the sensitivity for having their imagination touched off." Similarly, Barrow (1988, p. 89) points out the difficulty with enhancing the imagination if it is not already present in some form. An "important negative point is that developing imagination is not a matter of getting hold of `it' and training it, exercising it, or otherwise giving it room to roam. For 'it' does not exist until we are some way along the path of developing it, and even then 'it' exists only figuratively."

After some discussion on the topic, the high school math teacher modified her stance somewhat, by saying that imagination could probably be developed through classroom instruction. She feels that when a teacher knows the subject matter well there is more room for imagination: "Imagination in the classroom is derived from mastery of subject, and an interest in related areas." This echoes Barrow's (1988, p. 89) point of developing the imagination in context: "We have to get people to be imaginative about something, since the notion of having imagination that takes no specific form is incoherent. We therefore have to develop it by means of developing understanding of particular matters."

There is talk in the college community of not granting education degrees as undergraduate majors. Instead students would be encouraged to get a liberal arts degree in an area of interest with a fifth year of graduate study when they would specialize in education and take methods classes. I am not sure if the structure matters so much. Taking education classes and field experiences early helps some students to decide if this is really the profession they desire. But, I do wholeheartedly agree with the fact that students ought to take more interesting content classes than theoretical education classes.

A junior high teacher made suggestions for new courses to be added to the traditional education methods classes: "I think you would add tremendously to a college curriculum if you taught creative imagining and how that could be applied in the classroom. Maybe applied imagination. I think that's a really valid course."

A veteran elementary teacher, who is not certain that imagination can be taught, feels that a framework of broad goals can be set: "There are some things you can teach. Maybe it's philosophy. That you can teach. If somebody really internalizes those things and buys into it, then that has to affect their behavior. That will allow them to be more imaginative and intuitive in their teaching. It's the person I am that lets me be the teacher I am." Likewise, Barrow (1988, p. 89) suggests some philosophical opening up as a means to enhance the imagination. The reasoning given is that "since imagination involves conceiving of the unusual and effective, and since to be imaginative involves being both able and inclined to engage in such conceptualization, common sense suggests that opening the mind to the myriad customs, explanations, theories, problems, practices, values, and beliefs of human beings throughout history may serve to encourage both that inclination and ability."

A college teacher gave succinct advice for encouraging imaginative teaching: "Very simply to teach the 'I.' To teach that one cannot lose the 'I' or all is lost. To teach the exact antithesis of what is generally taught." A sound understanding of your own ego supersedes any recipe-like system of methods that you might adopt. In order to enable ourselves to apply suggestions we must know ourselves and glean the ideas suited to our unique personalities. Just as we can not dole out worksheets and expect our students to comprehend from a rendering of facts, we can not expect teachers to be handed worksheets of understanding. We all must make our own connections.

Perhaps a course in using your imagination in the classroom begins with teaching the "I" or taking stock of who I am as a teacher. What is it about me that makes me unique in my classroom demeanor? This would be an interesting question to ponder with a group of classroom teachers, since so often we rehearse our similarities with each other. An inherent part of being imaginative is being uniquely creative. It is therefore often difficult to conceive of how to teach an individual to be imaginative and why so many people shrug and simply say "You either are or you aren't."

We are all born with the capacity to be imaginative. We all have imaginations. I believe we can teach and enhance teachers' use of their imaginations. If we are to teach or encourage teachers to be imaginative, it is necessary to have them get in touch with their distinguishing characteristics. No one else can see through your eyes and a good understanding of how you view reality is an excellent springboard for creatively adapting your views and ideas. The group process of a class or discussion group is a wonderful vehicle for enhancing the understanding of what makes one unique. While sharing and comparing brings out similarities, such focused comparison can also provide the participants with discernment of distinguishing characteristics, a perception of who "I" am as distinct from the others. With a true appreciation for your uniqueness comes a sense of purpose. Confidence in your originality fosters creativity and the use of imagination.

When can you fit such a class into your busy schedule as a teacher? Perhaps inservice days could be an adequate beginning for this process. Many teachers agree that good inservice workshops are rare. Quite a few teachers feel that for such a workshop to be beneficial it needs to be at least a day long. Continued follow-up is also essential for lasting value. I have taught many staff development workshops. I have found that the structure of a class where participants are expected to attend once a week for a duration of a month or two, with assignments to try out ideas in their classrooms, is an excellent approach. There is the built-in support and the expectation that all will be attempting some change in their classrooms. The follow-up sharing on a weekly basis provides the needed encouragement.

Many are finding that there need not be "experts" called in to run the workshop and follow-up, but rather that teachers themselves have a lot to offer each other. An interested group of teachers could start their own support group and structure it as they choose. They could utilize research articles and the experiences of themselves and others as catalysts. Peer coaching affords an excellent form of follow-up support.

Teachers can learn a lot from each other through collaborative meetings where they share teaching methods. A good way to share is to have teachers demonstrate by having the other faculty members go through portions of the activities planned for students. Referring to this type of sharing, one teacher said that this is useful: "So we'd all be cross-pollinated as much as we can . . . I think one of the things we're talking about is being able to get outside your own frame of reference and to understand that somebody else's is as valid as yours." For example, a teacher who is particularly adept at storytelling could lead a group of teachers through some related activities. I suggested this to one such teacher who regularly gives workshops to teachers in the art of storytelling: "I like to start a storytelling workshop with family histories. Because we all have families and reminiscences, it's an easy way to talk about ourselves and lapse into storytelling. I think I might put them through a guided imagery experience, picturing the home of their childhood or a relative, or family treasures. Or ask them to concentrate on a child they have the most problem with or something like that. Imagine ways to work with or help the child. They might have some interesting ideas on positive ways to help. It's a way of getting them to use imagining."

Within the discussion of the theme of "storytelling" it was indicated that Egan (1986, 1988b) views the telling of a story from memory as an imaginative process. He has delineated a framework for organizing content into story form. He suggests that teachers utilize this schema when planning units of study. This mode is one way to expand a teacher's use of imagination. Whether a teacher follows Egan's "Story Form Framework" or simply extracts the basic idea of organization of subject matter in such a way that it can be "told" within an engaging story context, the teacher would surely enhance her use of imagination in teaching. This idea could be incorporated into graduate education classes or preservice teacher training as novice teachers learn how to compose units of study in varying disciplines.

Certainly inservice workshops on "storytelling as teaching" could be structured to enhance any teacher's use of imagination in daily classroom activities. I have taught such storytelling workshops and found them to be a delightful way to structure discussions of imaginative teaching. There are video tapes of professional storytellers that can be borrowed from local libraries. Some of the video tapes have the professionals giving performance tips. Such tapes could easily be incorporated into a teacher support group's discussions if there were no one else to run such a workshop. Taking control of your own inservice workshops can be easier than you might think. School district administrators are often delighted to get suggestions from teachers. They usually have the resources to provide the needed structure for relevant workshops and can often arrange for college credit for proposed classes.

Sharing by doing is much more meaningful than simply explaining, however any form of sharing is helpful. Teachers often feel isolated within their own classrooms, sharing ideas is always beneficial. It is an excellent way to stretch your own imagination because you come to realize different approaches and ways to get concepts across. Observing one another in action in the classroom is an excellent way to spark ideas. You can not help but imagine how you might do something differently, or if something you observe will work as well in your own situation. One award winning high school teacher mentioned particular techniques that he has observed in other teachers. Even though he is a veteran teacher, he was glad to adopt some of these wonderful techniques as his own. Therefore, he would encourage more sharing and exposure to imaginative techniques as the best means to foster imagination in teachers at any level of experience. The academy of educators that he belongs to as a Golden Apple award winner, has proposed to make video tapes of Golden Apple winners in action to share with other teachers: "So many of the Golden Apple teachers, just as one sample group, use imaginative techniques. It's the thing that tends to link us together." One teacher, feeling the problem of isolation, agreed that there is not enough time allowed for collaborative engagement: "That is one way of looking at what's amiss . . . There's so little contact and connection with each other, so we don't engage our own minds with each other."

One teacher thinks that it is more critical to spark imagination in veteran teachers rather than in new teachers. She feels that new teachers "want to try a lot of different things, they're very open, they're not set in their ways." Whereas veteran teachers often get regimented and tend to do something the same way without giving it much thought, let alone engaging their imaginations. I have observed many teachers over the years and I do not think there is anything particularly less imaginative about a teacher who has gained some experience in the field. Some of the most imaginative teachers I have encountered had been teaching for more than fifteen years. I think it has a lot more to do with personality than age or experience.

Recognition by peers and administrators provides needed support. Administrators do a lot to encourage or thwart imaginative teaching. Principals, in particular, set the tone for their school. A teacher who is self-motivated and highly imaginative may feel freer to work under a principal with a laissez faire attitude than an overbearing regimented leader. However the ideal setting would be with a principal who has genuine care, concern and respect for the students and faculty. Such an administrator finds time to spend in the classrooms, getting to know the teachers and students on a daily basis to understand the everyday occurrences, the successes and failures. Valuable support comes from more than just an occasional pat on the back. Encouragement is an ongoing process. Just as good teachers nurture their students on a daily basis, it is necessary for a conscientious administrator to demonstrate continuing concern with the teachers entrusted to his care. If a principal values imaginative teaching, this will be more prevalent in his school. District level administrators can have a similar influence.

As an illustration of how to encourage imaginative teaching, an administrator recounted an interesting example of a workshop she ran for a group of veteran public school teachers when she was working for an arts-in-education organization:

> We had four days—an intensive workshop . . . I had four artists who were doing the teaching. What we had decided together to do was to take one of the Mastery Learning (an unimaginative system of teaching language arts and mathematics to promote better scoring on standardized tests, mandated in the school system in the early 1980s) units which the teachers so loathed, but we had to find a way to make it meaningful . . . and make something connective out of it . . . we decided to do it in the disciplines that were represented, which were dance, visual art, writing, and theater . . . So the first day, the teachers were delighted—this was play time. The second day—'What are we going to teach?' (slams fist into hand) . . . The teacher wanted to know 'Why are we doing this?—I mean playing's all very well, but we've got to teach. What are we going to teach?' . . . we were stuck in, what I call the 'heuristic gap.' It's not me, it's Michael Polanyi's idea. (Polanyi 1962) That gap is between external definition and internal definition. The teachers were looking for external definition and I wasn't going to give it to them. So the second day was tense and everybody was ill-tempered and it was a bad day . . . The third day the very teacher who had said 'We want to be given stuff' was the first one to say 'Oh!' and it was all of course OK after that. The fourth day nobody wanted to leave because everybody was connected to everybody else . . . that makes me want to cry . . . it was distilled. It was like when you see all the theory that you've always known to be true, when you see it work in the most

concentrated possible fashion, so that everything that happens, happens passionately and truthfully. From the play time the first day, to the doubt and anger the second day, and the dropping off the face of the universe into nothing. Then the third day the discovery of connection. There's nothing so beautiful in the bloody world as a moment at which connection happens, any kind of connection: sexual, imaginative, human. And it's all the same thing . . . You see together. There's a moment when you know you're alive, and everybody there—you know you're alive together. That's why nobody wanted to leave Thursday, because we all knew we were alive together. That is what it's all about.

The meaning of a particular manner of presentation must be internalized, understanding at a superficial level will not suffice. Theoretical cognizance is not enough to nurture a teacher's use of her imagination. It is imperative to work through the process. As one college teacher put it: "You can't teach them process, through teaching them theory. You have to allow them to drop off the edge of the cliff and to find the intrinsic meaning for themselves because nothing else will do."

Whether the occurrence is as traumatic as dropping off a cliff or not is not the important metaphor here, but there comes a time of realization in this basic heuristic inner and outer exchange. It involves a gentle leading, rather than pushing, adroit questioning rather than blatant directing and a grasp of the notion of control. Control is a complicated entity—too much or too little can have disastrous results. The only one who can truly empower a person is himself. Others can provide encouragement and support and certainly stir an individual toward appropriate paths. But the ultimate goal is to travel the route of understanding and gain the insight for oneself. You can walk together, even hold each other's hands, occasionally leaning on one another for support, but each person must ultimately take the steps on his own.

Teachers need to search themselves first and then take their understanding to their students. It is essential for teachers to first take their own learning on their own terms in order to be able to teach students to do the same. An interactive classroom environment needs to be established. Teachers ought to explore their own natural excitement of discovery and learning. They need to engage the child in them. All too often we suggest that teachers put aside the child in them, they need to be "professional," or have a certain demeanor. Really, they need to teach from that child. To be that excited and sometimes silly self who loves this process of learning.

Preservice education has a lot to do with shaping the attitudes and values of beginning teachers. Imaginative college teachers who bring theory to life in education methods classes can have a beneficial effect on these budding young teachers. I have seen such a wonderful turn around in the content of education classes since I went through them in undergraduate school more than twenty years ago. It is interesting to note that many of the teachers I interviewed and observed who have been in the field at least as long as I, still believe that such classes are all unimaginative and theoretical with little hint of the practical aspects of teaching. One teacher who typically has at least one student teacher in her classroom each year put it like this: "Everything is pretty much theoretical in their classes or they've been given lock-step recipes to follow. Not much attention has been given to all the thought behind the action . . . More attention should be given to the process." The field experience components in colleges of education are the most valuable aspects of the course work. It is necessary for education classes to be taught using imaginative techniques because, as Barrow (1988, p. 90) indicates, classes are "taught in an imaginative way, so that much that cannot be taught may be caught." It is essential for universities and colleges of education to value the imagination in teaching in order to foster that in beginning teachers.

Barrow (1988, p. 89) mentions that "if we want people to develop imagination, we have to develop their understanding . . ." It is necessary for teachers to understand the process of teaching in general, let alone the specifics of what it means to be "an imaginative teacher." Cultivating the idea of teaching imaginatively makes little sense if one merely has a theoretical view of what teaching is all about. There is a necessity to be involved with teaching at the practical level in order to enhance one's teaching in an imaginative direction. As Barrow (1988, p. 89) indicates: "the understanding and embryonic imagination have to be developed in particular contexts."

Modeling is an important thing to do for youngsters, and also for teachers. If we are attempting to foster imagination in teaching, a reasonable approach to use with teachers is to have them observe, in action, what it is that you are referring to. Modeling for and observing other teachers is an excellent means of teaching and learning new classroom methods and techniques as long as there is adequate time allowed for collaborative discussions in pre and post conferencing. Peer coaching provides an excellent framework as such.

Modeling is important for student teachers. Many of us are privileged not only to influence the next generation with a class full of students but also have the opportunity to influence future generations through supervising student teachers and being observed by other preservice teachers. Most colleges and departments of education have criteria set up so that students observe in a wide variety of settings. Teaching styles vary with teachers' personalities. It is important to see diverse methods and techniques. It is essential that preservice teachers have many opportunities to interact and teach whole classes, small groups and individuals of different ages in various settings. Student teaching in the context of a classroom with an imaginative teacher is one of the best ways to promote the use of the imagination in preservice teachers. One veteran primary teacher I spoke with has at least one student teacher every year. To her modeling is taken for granted. She also advocates a balance between finding a comfort level and being coerced to grow: "It's also important to model that kind of teaching for them. It is necessary to always get feedback from them as to how they're feeling about things so that they can find a comfortable style. But I think we all need to be stretched to reach our potential." Another imaginative high school teacher is in full agreement with the idea of modeling good teaching behavior in order to foster it: "In terms of imagination, one of the things that can be done is just exposing students to more imaginative teaching techniques. We tend to model the first teacher that we worked with as a student teacher. We tend to model teachers we had in high school or especially in college. Exposing them to really imaginative techniques and showing openness to that, is probably going to be the single most useful way of teaching imagination."

Another veteran intermediate teacher who has worked with many student teachers feels that the best way to teach someone is to model for them: "In my opinion, the way to make someone a better teacher is just to give them so much love and support. They will then teach their children that way . . . You have to teach them by interacting with them in the way you want them to interact . . . You can't say 'Go back and read child growth and development.' To teach the student teacher we put them in with a master teacher."

Viewing video taped lessons is one way to model aspects of teaching. One high school teacher advocates much more time be devoted to the practical aspects of day to day classroom instruction. This is best accomplished by placing preservice teachers in school settings in order to see various approaches and teaching styles: "I think that imagination can really be modeled in a lot of ways. I'd love to put together . . . a series of those video tapes." Such video tapes could provide modeling for experienced teachers as well as student teachers. Teachers who could not otherwise go into a colleague's classroom to observe might be able to watch video taped lessons followed up with discussion with fellow teachers. Video tapes can be fast forwarded to forgo mundane aspects of daily teaching and replayed over and over to catch subtle nuances of a teacher's performance one might otherwise miss.

Simple observation is not enough. It is important to let teachers be aware of the thought processes that go into imaginative teaching. Just as imaginative classroom teachers use the technique of "wondering aloud" to help young students understand some mental processes, this should be done in a similar way with teachers who are observing. This requires a dedicated colleague who is willing to take the time to open up some of her thought processes to others. This involves more than merely telling the teachers what you were thinking, but just as you would probe the students in the classroom setting, ask appropriate leading questions to draw out ideas and imagine along with the other teachers.

Asking a student teacher to picture what might happen in a given situation she is planning for would help to encourage imaginative planning and probably instill some confidence by enabling the student teacher to gain some familiarity with a situation she has not yet encountered. Thereby providing the student teacher with a resource to draw upon. I suggested this use of guided imagery to a cooperating teacher. She reacted favorable: "I really like the idea of asking her to picture what might happen in the classroom, and talk through what she sees as a way to develop imagining. She'll be more comfortable when one of her predictions transpires, or starts out but then goes off on a tangent or whatever. The act of having her picture all that could happen in the classroom will help her practice imagining. Then because she will have had those trial runs, she'll be more comfortable when she's doing the actual teaching and maybe freer to go with her intuitions."

A high school teacher suggests asking preservice teachers to come up with a variety of ways to teach each lesson as a way to expand their imaginative planning abilities: "Here's a lesson, try and come up with three different creative approaches to teach that . . . General Patton, not somebody we often associate with higher education, once had a quote along the lines of 'Never tell somebody what to do. Tell them what you want done, and then let them amaze you with what they're able to do.' I'd like to see more of that."

Viewing the familiar in unfamiliar ways, or coming up with as many variations of approach to teaching a particular idea, appears to be an excellent means for stretching and expanding teachers' imaginations. Devising several techniques for teaching the same lesson is a creative act. Obviously, imaging is occurring mentally as the teacher ponders the possibilities. This is an opening up exercise to look at things in new, unusual, and thus, imaginative ways. It is important to note that inventive behavior may have some inherent anxiety for many teachers, "since creation involves a risk of failure" (Rubin 1985, p. 34). Thus, it is extremely important that such an exercise be done in a supportive climate. Indeed, if imagination is truly to be cultivated in teachers, any small inclination toward its expansion should be recognized and applauded.

Relaxation is a necessary ingredient for promoting imagination. Winter, spring, and summer vacations are all essential factors for maintaining the necessary energy to teach imaginatively on a daily basis. One imaginative, energetic, veteran high school math teacher of over thirty years insists that getting away to her cottage by a lake in another state each summer is paramount to her successful teaching career: "It is amazing how much you absorb by senses when you relax!" She suggested non-academic workshops as possibilities to enhance teachers' imagination and intuition: "Maybe we should organize fun groups to move out of pencil and paperizing. Walks in the woods—What do you see?—What do you think you see?—What do you hear? What does it sound like?—Is there an aroma in the woods?—Where have you experienced it before? Cycling trips—Where should we go? Why?—What will we see?—How will we feel when we get there?—Did we see what we expected? More, or less? You could expand *any* typically non-academic experience into a never forgotten lesson in intuition and imagination!"

The idea of modeling imaginative teaching is an excellent starting point for discussion and for teachers' individual connection making. Observing an imaginative lesson in person or on tape could provide the necessary spark which can then be kindled. Once the fire of imagination is set it spreads quickly and is hard to put out. If a teacher has the fire of imagination burning in her soul, she is able to truly educate—to lead out from the darkness into the light. The blaze of the imagination provides that light!

Promoting the Use of Intuition with Teachers

Many of the same techniques that apply to enhancing teachers' use of imagination certainly pertain to fostering their use of intuition. Modeling, observing and sharing are helpful for promoting an understanding of intuition in the classroom. But, as has been pointed out, intuition is best enhanced by experience.

Intuitive thinking is learnable through experience and a careful effort to process perceptual evidence. By actively looking for clues, speculating about their meaning, and testing the resulting hunches, intuitive thought is cultivated. In making intuitive decisions, attention is focused on the total problem rather than an isolated part. Practiced regularly, it produces intellectual rules of thumb which facilitate teaching efficiency. (Rubin 1985, p. 69)

We are reminded of the spiraling effect that experience has on the ability to come up with useful intuitive insights. Being open to such experience is the crucial factor to begin with. But as one gains more experience in general and more experience with the specific aspects of using intuition in teaching, the more confidence one has in the intuitive mode and the more open one is to its utilization. Being able to discuss the process with a sympathetic veteran teacher can be extremely beneficial for a novice teacher.

So is it possible to teach someone to be intuitive? Intuition, just as imagination, is something which we all possess. Successfully using your intuition in the classroom largely depends on trusting your own instincts and feelings. This sounds like an easy thing to accomplish but can actually be difficult for many teachers. If one constantly looks to a higher authority for definitive answers to questions of technique and discipline in the classroom, it may seem peculiar to display the confidence in yourself to respond to situations on a daily basis. If for years your reactions have strictly been "by the book" then you may not be reacting intuitively, but rather responding the way you feel that others would like.

As was suggested in the section on promoting the use of imagination, it is likewise important to get in touch with your own uniqueness to facilitate your openness to intuitive insights. If you are not accustomed to reacting intuitively, then the most difficult aspect might be simply to trust your instincts. Often teachers are hesitant to rely on their inner feelings because of doubt or insecurity. Confidence is paramount to intuitive teaching. Trust in your abilities and confidence in your instincts will allow you to be open to intuition. Experience tends to give us more confidence in ourselves. So is intuition something we just wait for? Is it possible to teach someone to be intuitive? Again we are all intuitive, it is merely a matter of tapping our own resources through trusting ourselves and the knowledge we possess. It does get easier with time and experience.

We can foster confidence in teachers and assist them in becoming more open to their intuitions. Sharing is a most helpful tool to facilitate this. We need to build in time for teachers to get together to talk among themselves. It is particularly important for novice teachers to be able to bring their concerns to experienced teachers who would be willing to help them. Teachers need to share their successes and any frustrations they might have. We need to encourage teachers to develop the technique of self-observation so that they can cue into intuitive reactions they might have as lessons are in progress.

One difference with fostering intuition rather than imagination lies in the emphasis on the students more so than the subject matter. It seems that thorough knowledge of the content area tends to free a teacher to be more imaginative with teaching the subject. And whereas one could also argue that familiarity of subject matter can make a teacher more intuitive regarding the content of lesson, this may not enhance a teacher's intuitive reactions to the students. It is the familiarity with one's students that allows a teacher to develop useful insights during classroom presentation. Teachers need to develop the technique of kid watching (Goodman 1985) so that they are not so much concerned with the content but rather, how students are reacting. They need to be able to pick up on the subtle cues given them by the students and learn how to use these cues to modify the experience or activities on the spur of the moment.

As with promoting the use of imagination, it is also important to model the use of intuition in teaching. Such observations, of course, need to be followed up with conferencing since many aspects of the use of intuition are not readily apparent. One veteran teacher who was speaking in reference to her work with a student teacher said: "It's important for them to observe what happens in the classroom. If something comes up that's of interest to the kids, I notice that and go with it. I take suggestions from the students. You should point out how lively and interesting a discussion can be when you let the kids take the lead and you're just there encouraging them, but not directing them."

Many cues from students are not vocalized. Techniques that enhance one's ability to pick up on subtle behavioral clues in the classroom are important. A teacher suggested a checklist to assist with such identification as teachers observe in classrooms: "I think that something that might be helpful when they're first coming in to observe would be to have a checklist on seeing the non-verbal kinds of communication. Find examples of children who have become inattentive, what are the signs to look for there, and what are ways to bring them back in. Have discussions with them. When can you tell that a kid just isn't understanding something and how to stop and reexplain it. Try to get him aboard rather than just going along. Those are things that beginning teachers can learn, be made more conscious of. I think it might be helpful too, for them to see that those things are occurring in me, a veteran teacher, conducting the class, for them to realize that no one ever stops learning."

Another confident, experienced, intuitive teacher believes that the way to start teaching someone how to be more intuitive in the classroom is by redefining teaching for the teacher and then work from there: "I think the way to do it is you have to go back to the idea that teaching is a conversation rather than an objective and an evaluation. It's like the mother with the child or you with your friend. It's a communication process . . . First you have to start by defining what teaching *is*. How do you make it better? You have to do that by just coming to their normal life, as if you were trying to show your friend how to do something. What is the process? Part of that process is listening to your friend when she says 'I don't understand this.' I took three courses with Bettleheim (Bruno Bettleheim at the University of Chicago). Loved it! What the man told me is that 'Children have something to say. Listen to children.' . . . The looking in their faces, that's part of this communication. It's interactive . . . It's an art! What you're looking at is not the skill of teaching. You're looking at the art of teaching."

It is indeed the art of teaching we are talking about throughout the discussions of teachers' use of their imaginations and intuitions. The inspired sort of teaching that comes from the soul more than it comes from the intellect is a difficult entity to teach. There are skills involved that we can point out, but it is not a predesignated system that you can simply adopt and implement in your classroom. As with any art, learning and practicing the skills are an important aspect of becoming proficient, however it is not until the skills and techniques no longer get in the way and you are able to produce beautiful renditions of art work in your own style that you have truly mastered the art not just the craft. So too, when teachers follow the song in their hearts they are able to create exciting experiences with their students. Beginning teachers need a lot of support to help them continue to work through their tenuous qualms of doubt and uncertainty. These feelings can be so consuming that there is little room for intuition to surface. It is unfair for us to expect them to be in touch with the students and the students' feelings if they are not given enough support to help them work through their own feelings.

An intuitive high school teacher believes that "intuition can be developed by classroom instruction." She feels that reading body language and facial expressions is something that "students could be trained to be aware of." But she thinks that beginning teachers are too insecure to be spontaneous: "I think it takes a very secure person in the classroom to achieve the ability to roam all over and pick up on things as they come. I don't think new teachers are ever that secure when they first start."

A junior high teacher feels that knowledge of the particular age group in terms of child development is important to a teacher's use of intuition in the classroom: "Part of intuition is being able to perceive how the students are picking something up, how they're interpreting something. What messages are the students sending to you? You have to be able to understand why they are saying verbally or nonverbally what they're saying. You need to understand the students' level of development. How I respond to sixth graders is completely different than my intuitive reactions to eighth graders." This teacher further suggests that a teacher needs to really know his classes and how each class functions as a group. He feels that instruction in group dynamics would be helpful to encourage teachers' use of intuition: "You need knowledge of group dynamics, knowledge of how your group works with each other and functions as a group. Knowing the personality of the group and what kinds of things motivate the kids is important." Another high school teacher also feels that intuition stems from really knowing your students well. He thinks that openness is the important attribute to acquire to be intuitive: "I think most intuition for good teachers really can be taught if they learn to be open and they learn to be observant . . . the idea of how to read your students needs to be taught and talked about so that they've got a context in which to put the information later when they do start noticing that certain things always happen. I was fortunate during my student teaching that one of my supervisory teachers was a wonderfully intuitive teacher. That helped me . . . We would sit and talk . . . about what it was that he saw. Obviously, I learned a lot from working with him."

Again, modeling the behavior you would like to foster is an effective way to teach it. Because of the complexity of the intuitive process, and because it appears to depend a lot on your level of confidence and experience, many feel that certain elements of the process can be taught to new teachers, but that much encouragement is needed during the first few years of teaching as much of the art is being assimilated into the essence of each new teacher as a person. Intuition is not rational. Often the logical mind has a tendency to reject intuition. An open person says there must be a reason for feeling certain ways and is willing to explore such perceptions.

Teachers need to be aware of their own body language as well as that of their students. They need a true sense of themselves both mentally and as they appear physically to their students. Videotaping teachers in action can be helpful for them as a self-evaluation tool. They can assess their demeanor for themselves. One high school teacher says that he has used an article "called 'What Is Your Body Language Telling Your Students?' A lot of teachers don't know how they're coming across or how they sound." Once you have a good sense of yourself you can move from being self-conscious to being conscious of your students and the messages they are putting out in subtle, nonverbal cues. This newly defined consciousness will enable a teacher to intuitively respond not only to signals from the students but also to pick up on environmental stimuli that might enhance or detract from the transpiring learning experience.

An intuitive high school teacher suggests that too often teachers of that age group unwittingly interrogate students through inopportune questioning: "They need to learn how to read their students. It's very, very easy to put students on the defensive. Once you do, the students don't want to respond to you. I see so many student teachers who put their students on the defensive just because of the questions they ask. They studied Bloom's taxonomy (Bloom 1956) to know how to ask questions on different levels of subject matter. But they don't necessarily learn how to ask different questions on a personal level. So there's a lot that can be done that way that will help to foster the use of intuition in the classroom."

Besides more reflective observation of good teachers who operate in the intuitive mode and discussion of what is seen, more emphasis on the psychological realm is needed to promote the use of intuition in teaching. It is necessary for a teacher to be in touch with her own feelings to be able to pick up on cues from the students. Enhancing one's sense of awareness in general, is warranted to foster a teacher's use of intuition. It is essential to strive for being attentive and being open. This seems to call for group discussion akin to therapy, seeking out and dispelling inhibitions and heightening one's perceptual ability and sensitivity. Some modified form of the "sensitivity training" popular in the 1960s might be utilized to enhance intuition.

Vaughan (1979) suggests exercises for "awakening intuition" that might be taken into account. "Exercises for developing the concentration necessary for awakening intuition work best when they are combined with relaxation training" (Vaughan 1979, p. 11). She suggests meditation and breathing exercises for such relaxation to "allow your mind to be quiet and clear" (Vaughan 1979, p. 14). She further suggests an "awareness exercise" to attend to one's own physical sensation as well as one for inner awareness and various forms of "concentration" and "receptivity" exercises. Vaughan (1979, p. 15) describes in detail "one of the most effective methods of combining body awareness and imagination for deep relaxation and the enhancement of intuitive faculties (which) has been developed by Lester Fehmi of the Princeton Medical Center. He calls it the *Open Focus* exercise (Fehmi 1975). It consists of a series of questions about your ability to imagine certain experiences without making any effort to achieve them." Certainly such exercises are not inherent to the specifics of using intuition in teaching, however, imagination and intuition are deeply imbedded in a person as a human being. So obviously any enhancement in these areas will carry over into teaching.

Reinterpreting the Encouragement of Imagination and Intuition

The heuristic internal and external interchange of ideas is helpful to promote imaginative and intuitive teaching. The word "heuristic" has been used alternately with "interpretation," "re-interpretation" and "discovery" (Polanyi 1962). Polanyi (1962, p. 77) tells us that "Intellectual acts of a heuristic kind make an *addition* to knowledge . . . " When referring to the interchange between external and internal awareness, I am using "heuristic" to connote a continually re-interpreted comprehension and enhanced discovery of additional knowledge of self.

One way to promote imaginative teaching is to use the process of sharing teaching methods by having faculty members teach each other, brainstorm and discuss their techniques. It is refreshing and enlightening to be able to get outside of your own frame of reference and to understand that somebody else's is as valid as yours, thus calling into play the external and internal communication among self and others.

I have referred to the idea of being outside oneself while one is teaching. The teacher needs to be the one conducting the lesson, but also needs to be the one observing it all. Helping student teachers to be their own observers is a way of promoting the student teacher's use of imagination and intuition, by looking within for critique. Having a student teacher picture what might happen in the classroom and talking through what she sees is a way to develop imagining. She will be more comfortable when one of her predictions transpires. Having her picture what could happen in the classroom will help her practice imagining. Because she will have had those internal trial runs, she will be more comfortable when she is doing the actual teaching and might be freer to go with her intuitions. If these mental rehearsal techniques were practiced regularly by a student teacher with an imaginative, intuitive cooperating teacher, the student teacher would develop her imaginative and intuitive capacities in a meaningful way. A mentor can be a helpful guide for discussion of imagined scenarios during planning.

Intuition is best enhanced through experience. Enhancement of one's intuitive ability in the classroom stems from general life experience and getting to know yourself better. It is a heuristic encounter of inner feelings as you begin to see repeated patterns. Intuition is intensified not only from knowing students better and seeing repeated patterns, but also through opening up to know yourself better. It is through the internal and external heuristic encounter that intuition is fostered.

Not only does the teacher need to be open to this heuristic encounter to free oneself intuitively and imaginatively, but also the locus of this feeling of freedom is partially within the teacher but it is also external. The administration needs to encourage imaginative teaching.

The heuristic interchange between external and internal definition plays an important part in the promotion or discouragement of teachers' use of intuition and imagination. We cannot simply define "how to teach" through formulas, systems and packaged methods. That definition must come from the heart and soul of the teacher involved in the process of perfecting the art of teaching. We need to wrestle with our changing perceptions and explanations in order to make sense of the complicated processes we continue to employ and those processes we choose to add to our repertoire. If a teacher is asking for external definition and a wise mentor is refusing to hand it over but encouraging the teacher to continue to struggle for self interpretation, then there comes a time of being stuck in the "heuristic gap" (Polanyi 1962) between external definition and internal definition. With perseverance the teacher will come to take learning on her own terms. Once she makes the switch to an internal definition of teaching and looks within she is able to connect. Understanding is hers because she makes it hers, it cannot be handed over.

A shift in one's thinking, a basic heuristic inner and outer exchange, might be urged for teachers who are overly concerned with how they are perceived in the classroom. This type of interpretation is intended to bring one from being self-conscious to being conscious of self and others.

Both external and internal resources are valuable and need to be tapped. Some of the external resources available to teachers are in the form of books and equipment. Other people and ideas passed on through writing, conversation, observation, etc. can be included as available resources for teachers. The available resources within oneself are also called into play daily. The conjuring up of ideas is using one's internal resources. Often internal and external resources are combined as teachers internalize new ideas. If a heuristic balance is achieved, one external resource will probably conjure *many* internal resources for meaningful use.

Teachers must focus outside themselves to be conscious of students' needs and understandings without losing the consciousness of self. The heuristic interchange is a constant process of balancing. This is a common imaginative and intuitive mode which good teachers employ daily, while planning, instructing and evaluating.

There are available methods for encouraging the imagination and intuition, the more important element to keep in mind when considering promoting imagination and intuition in teaching is the valuing of these modes or characteristics. Valuing imagination and intuition enhances a teacher's security to implement creative ideas and to trust in her intuition. It is important to value the use of imagination and intuition for yourself. Likewise, this valuing by administrators and authority figures is an important element towards cultivating and promoting the teachers' everyday use of imagination and intuition.

What value do you place on using your imagination and intuition in the classroom? Do you feel secure in these areas? How could you enhance your own use of imagination and intuition?

CHAPTER 9

ENHANCING STUDENTS' IMAGINATION AND INTUITION

The debt we owe to the play of imagination is incalculable.

—Carl Gustav Jung in
Psychological Types (1923, p. 82)

Although this book has been concerned with the way teachers use their imaginations and intuition, it makes sense to take a brief look at how to cultivate student imagination and intuition in the classroom. There is a reciprocal nature to the teaching and learning processes. It takes an imaginative teacher to enhance a child's imagination. Likewise, a teacher needs a personal understanding of intuition to encourage that mode of learning in her students.

In this chapter I survey some of the literature written regarding how to encourage students to be more imaginative and intuitive.

The 1960s was a decade that saw a surge of classroom activities involving creativity. Courses in creativity were taught as part of the teacher training program at some universities. Torrance and Torrance (1973) reviewed 142 experiments in elementary and secondary schools which were designed to assist students to develop creative thinking. These experiments were all conducted between 1960 and the time of the study. Torrance (1977) calls the 1960s a subtle revolution. "This revolution has been in the direction of greater emphasis on both creative problem solving and creative expression" (Torrance 1977, p. 5). Torrance (1977) suggests ways that teachers can foster creativity in students by, providing opportunities for creative behavior, developing skills for creative learning, rewarding creative achievements, and establishing creative relationships with children.

Torrance (1977, pp. 26-27) delineates eight specific things that teachers can do to enhance creativity in their students:

1. Give purpose to creative writing.

2. Provide experiences which make children more sensitive to environmental stimuli.

3. Develop a constructive attitude toward the information sought.

4. Provide adequate warm-up for creative activities.

5. In warming-up pupils for creative thinking, avoid giving examples or illustrations which will freeze or unduly shape their thinking.

6. Avoid giving evaluation comments too frequently during practice problems or activities.

7. Provide unevaluated (off-the-record) practice.

8. To evoke originality in thinking, make it clear that such thinking is expected and will be rewarded.

Researchers have looked into the use of certain types of questioning to promote imagination in students

(Barell 1980; Haley-Oliphant 1987; Hunter 1972). In his book, *Playgrounds of Our Minds*, John Barell (1980) provides us with what he calls the "imaginative questioning sequence." In this method of questioning the teacher starts with questions that look at factual knowledge: who? what? when? where? questions. The teacher would then progress to analytical questions that would ask: why? and with what effects? The next step would be to ask evaluative questions that elicit students' opinions. The last type of questioning is the imaginative. Imaginative questions ask "what if?" and have the students use supposition. Barell suggests this sequence for the study of history. For studying science, he suggests a similar line of questioning. The one deviation is the suggestion to use application questions with students when studying science, rather than the evaluative questions mentioned for studying history. He points out that there is no necessity to use such a progression with every question asked.

Alicia E. Haley-Oliphant (1987) did research in a junior high school science class with a particular teacher who used a technique that she called "Mind Games" to provoke students' imagination. Basic to this technique is the use of hypothetical questioning. Similar to Barell's suggestion of "imaginative questioning," the "Mind Games" technique utilizes open-ended, "what if?" questions. The teacher will often conjure the premise for the students and continue to question them as they respond. Haley-Oliphant points out that the teacher "shapes" the activity, but it is actually structured by the interaction of the teacher-student inquiry.

Barell (1980) argues that fantasy and daydreaming should be a regular part of elementary and secondary classroom learning. He says that teachers should purposefully cultivate the daydreams and imagination of their students. Barell is particularly adamant about promoting fantasy with adolescents. It is useful to have adolescents put themselves into roles and situations that they might one day encounter to help override the feeling of not yet being in control of their own lives. "Imagining possible futures and solutions is one means of confronting this feeling of powerlessness" (Barell 1980, p. 85). Barell suggests that teachers share their own fantasies with their students and invite the students to do the same. He suggests several ways that such sharing might take place, including informal discussion and writing.

Barell (1980) points out a number of ways to get students to use their imaginations in language arts activities. Some of these include: setting aside time "to let their minds wander," then having students fully describe the mental images; and visualizing scenes from literature.

Richard de Mille (1976) provides many examples of fantasy exercises which teachers may use to engage their students' imaginations. He suggests that the students might visualize a particular place with which they are familiar, students would then describe this environment to themselves in terms of the sights and sounds. Students would then be invited to alter the locale and rearrange its parts. In another example, de Mille suggests that teachers have their students think of a recent problem, then imagine themselves acting out a solution and examining the results. The examples are mainly in the area of language arts. De Mille encourages a lot of visualization and description, often resulting from stories or novels that students have read.

Barell (1980, p. 89) points out that imagining, daydreaming, visualizing, etc., should be done purposefully. It is important that the students understand that these modes of thought are valued and not frivolous:

> Any of the above suggestions should not be attempted without conscious purpose, that is, their value is sub-

stantively lost on the young dreamers if these activities are not part of an on-going attempt to upgrade the value placed upon the powers of imagination, specifically upon daydreaming. To engage in these activities once or twice without follow-up, without leading to more advanced forms of explorating daydreams and their extent and possible meanings, is to waste time and is only a half-hearted attempt to recognize a significant cognitive process.

Torrance and Meyers (1970) agree that fostering imagination and creativity in children must be a deliberate endeavor.

Margaret B. Sutherland (1971) suggests the need to be able to control or discipline the imagination. She feels that this is one of the objectives of education, "if imagination is to be creatively or valuably used, experimental work on role-playing, simulation techniques, etc., suggests the need for some addition of intelligent control" (Sutherland 1971, p. 192). She reminds educators that one of the best ways to promote imagination in children is to provide them with many diverse experiences. It is the experiences that are used as "raw material" for imagining. Sutherland argues that the range and variety of real experiences determine the boundaries to the scope of imagining.

Sutherland points out that teachers can stimulate students' imaginations through words. She reminds us that the teacher must provide for good understanding of verbal and written language, because it is through the use of words that one is able to express her imagination.

"Freedom to think" is another crucial factor in the development of the imagination in classrooms, according to Sutherland (1971). Students must be allowed to think and experiment freely. Students need to "find" their own solutions. Teachers need to respect students' solutions as valid, so as to minimize the fear of making mistakes.

> *Emotion is the chief source of all becoming-conscious. There can be no transforming of darkness into light and of apathy into movement without emotion.*
>
> —Carl Gustav Jung in
> *Psychological Aspects of the
> Modern Archetype* (1938)

Sutherland (1971) feels that although "emotional imagination" may be more difficult to encourage, it is nonetheless important that teachers are "educating the emotions" of their students. Sutherland suggests that teachers should help students discriminate among various emotions. She cautions that just evoking the emotions is not enough, "once the emotional response is there, how is it educated? Is its simple existence enough?" (Sutherland 1971, p. 201). She suggests that education of the emotions should produce individuals who are capable of controlling their emotions and who have a balanced view between emotion and behavior. She argues that educated individuals should be happier and healthier and able to cope with their emotions. There needs to be a feeling of achievement in learning to enhance a better emotional state. Sutherland provides us with four forms for the direct use of imagination to improve emotional states: "the development of the technique of turning attention to other situations when the present situation is unsatisfactory; the development of the technique of re-structuring an actual situation by thinking about it imaginatively; the development of greater imaginative insight into other people's points of view; and the use of imagination in planning" (Sutherland 1971, p. 206).

Sutherland cautions that educating imagination is a gradual process and must be thought of in general terms. Although she recognizes that individual lessons to foster imagination can be helpful, she feels that "the education of imagination is more pervasive and less directly controlled than lessons . . ." (Sutherland 1971, p. 209).

> Education can thus try to influence imagination both directly and indirectly; by directing it towards comprehension of other people's situations, by showing its use as alternative occupation, and by showing the possibility of arriving at new understanding of the individual's own situation; by providing also real experience of a kind which will contribute to future happiness and confidence as well as to future imaginative constructions . . . In some ways education has to be much more concerned with the general experience of the child than with developing detailed exercises of imagination or with specific subject teaching. It has also to be more concerned with these positive contributions than with possible censorship of allegedly undesirable stimulation of imagination. (Sutherland 1971, p. 209)

Ted Hughes (1988) argues for the use of myth and story in teaching to engage the students' imaginations. He says that the students should learn the stories to "take possession" of them so that they might "reenter the story at will" (Hughes 1988, p. 32). Hughes looks at each story as a "unit of imagination" or "a whole separate imagination." Each person can hold many such units. "In the attending to the world of such a story there is the beginning of imaginative and mental control" (Hughes 1988, p. 32). Hughes views the teaching of society's myths and stories as a major part of educating children. One word from such a well known story can conjure up the image of the entire story if it has been learned well. He offers this as a starting point to strengthening the imagination, which he believes to be a crucial function of education. However, he recognizes that this has been basically lacking in today's educational system. Hughes suggests looking toward the "inner world" as a key toward imaginative development. "All the lost awareness and powers and allegiance of our biological and spiritual being are there" (Hughes 1988, p. 41). The imagination is what connects our outer and inner worlds: "It is imagination that embraces both outer and inner worlds in a creative spirit" (Hughes 1988, p. 43). Hughes proposes that we follow in the footsteps of Plato and teach myths and legends as "ideal educational material," which lay out the "blueprints for imagination."

In his book *Teaching as Storytelling: An Alternative Approach to Teaching and Curriculum in the Elementary School* (1986) and a paper "Memory and Story in Teacher's Knowledge and Action" (1988b), Kieran Egan also advocates the use of story in education, however he discusses this use mainly from the standpoint of "teachers' knowledge and action" (Egan 1988b, p. 4). He provides teachers with curriculum planning ideas utilizing "story form framework" for various content matters. The presentation of subject matter in story form makes the content more engaging for students. He does mention similar ideas as Hughes in having students learn stories and myths. Egan feels that it is the memorization process that helps to develop the imagination. In his chapter "The Origins of Imagination and the Curriculum," Egan (1988a) espouses a similar view as Hughes. Egan looks at oral cultures and their use of story and myth as a way of keeping traditions alive through the telling of set stories. "The path from orality to literacy is one we want all children to take in our educational system" (Egan 1988a, p. 93). Egan attempts to rediscover "the kinds of thinking that have proven effective in cultures that do not have writing" (Egan 1988a, p. 95). The link here is that during early childhood there is an oral culture that develops. If teachers can tap into the imaginative thinking of the early years, the transition to literacy can be made smoothly, while retaining some of the valued thinking that goes with the oral tradition. For Egan, memory is an important aspect of the development of the imagination. It is through the remembering, participating in and conserving of the stories of our culture, that children expand their imaginations and have a base for further imaginings.

Gareth Matthews (1988) raises the question of evoking the "philosophical imagination" in children's literature. Although he does not offer explicit directions for teachers, the implicit understanding is to take care in selection of stories for children. He speaks to writers of children's literature and illustrates how "philosophical imagination can give richness and meaning to literature written for children" (Matthews 1988, p. 186). Matthews feels that it is important to address basic questions of philosophy in children's literature. In this way authors are showing respect for their young readers by not being condescending to them; "it is also a celebration of the humanity we share with our children" (Matthews 1988, p. 197).

Another proponent of the use of story, June Sturrock (1988) also advocates freedom and spontaneity for the child in educational endeavors. She is mainly concerned with the young child in her discussion of imagination in education. She looks at freedom in Wordsworth's terms as "the freedom of the imagination to roam, the freedom involved in self-forgetfulness, and the freedom given by the imagination's ability to apprehend and accept what the reason cannot grasp" (Sturrock 1988, p. 60). She likens Bruno Bettleheim to Wordsworth in that they both suggest the use of fairy tales to teach young children in imaginative ways about feelings and to "help the child to experience some mental freedom" (Sturrock 1988, p. 61). Sturrock uses characters and authors of prose and poetry to illustrate the need for developing children's imagination through education. Part of her underlying message is similar to

Hughes' argument for the use of story in teaching and learning, but she also points out the necessity for unorganized play situations and for individualistic treatment of youngsters in educational settings.

Otto Weininger (1988) agrees that "pretend play" in early childhood years is an essential aspect for the development of the imagination in children. It is during play that the child sets up hypotheses for himself to test out. Once tested, these concepts are then added to the child's "thinking repertoire" for further and higher levels of reality testing. Weininger makes a distinction between "what if" and "as if" pretend play. "Imagining—'what if'—is a solitary activity within the child's mind, and is only sometimes overheard in actual words. Pretending—'as if'—is usually done with other children, or, for the child who has no one with whom to play, with imaginary people or dolls" (Weininger 1988, p. 148). Weininger suggests that preschool teachers need to be good listeners and observers. He feels that it is equally important for the teacher to become part of the play with the child at the level displayed. He warns that the teacher should attempt to lead or organize the child's play. The teacher should be encouraging and try to extend, but not change the theme of the play that the child sets up. "The teacher observes and asks questions about what the child says, and helps to draw out information from the child, maintaining the theme provided by the child, but at a pace that allows the child to feel comfortable and pleased with the conversation" (Weininger 1988, p. 146). He also warns that teachers should recognize that young children will often use materials and props in a completely different manner than intended. As the children get older they will begin to use the material closer to its intention because they are gradually being able to understand symbolism. It is important for adults to interact with children but not to set the structure. "The teacher guides, but does not control; questions, but does not judge; answers, but does not criticize. By doing so the teacher fosters in the best possible ways the process of imagination, pretend play, and intellectual development in the children with whom he or she works" (Weininger 1988, p. 149).

Although his major concentration is on the psychological aspects of make-believe and imaginative play in young children, Jerome L. Singer (1973) speaks to some implications for later childhood education. Singer's idea of "make-believe " is the same as Weininger's "pretend play". They both use the same denotations and connotations when discussing the "as if" method of imaginative play in young children. Singer (1973, p. 245) notes "that there is a considerable continuing interest in make-believe activities and fantasy games which is largely suppressed" with children ages nine through thirteen. Singer admonishes the suppression of imaginative play in school age children. He argues that if it is fostered and channeled, school can be made more interesting for students. He recommends formal and informal dramatization as one aspect of utilizing students interest in make-believe play. This "undoubtedly will enhance their interest and the positive affect associated with school, but also will help generate greater elaborative skills in communication as well" (Singer 1973, p. 246). One of the aspects of socio-dramatic play that Singer mentions which is helpful for the school age child is that of role playing and role reversal. Tapping into this phase of imaginative play provides possibilities for deeper understanding in various subject areas. Singer mentions many positive aspects of enhancing make-believe thought for school age children including the fact that it will "help them develop their capacities for planning" (Singer 1973, p. 246). In a later work, Singer and Singer (1976) have compiled various exercises and techniques that teachers and parents might use to enhance imaginative play in children.

A variety of studies recognizing the importance of imaginative play have discussed ways to foster this process in children. Many of these studies deal with enhancing imaginative play in disadvantaged children (Freyberg 1973; Griffing 1974; Rosen 1974; Saltz, Dixon and Johnson 1977; Saltz and Johnson 1974; Smilansky 1973; Udwin and Shmuckler 1981). Some studies relate a technique sometimes termed "play tutoring" or modeling for enhancing imaginative play in children (Gottlieb 1973; Singer and Singer 1976; Smith, Dagleish and Herzmark 1981; Smith and Sydall 1978).

Maxine Greene (1978, 1988) proposes the use of the arts in general as main avenues to promote and enhance the development of the imagination in students. She sees the arts awakening "untapped possibilities" because "there are always new beginnings with the arts" (Greene 1988, p. 53). She views the engagement of students in a continual "quest for possibility" as the manner necessary for cultivating their imaginations. She offers no specifics, no recipes like Torrance or Barell, but rather suggests the need for opening, awakening, and questioning: "It is a question of opening subject matters as possible perspectives on the shared world, a question of releasing people for their own pursuits of meaning, their own searches for answers, their own efforts to name and articulate what they live" (Greene 1988, p. 52).

Robin Barrow (1988, p. 79) argues that the imagination is "by no means exclusively a concern of the arts." He feels that fostering students' imagination is an essential concern of education, but that its development can only occur indirectly "as a result of teaching certain kinds of curriculum subjects in a particular kind of way." Barrow sets the stage by going into various definitions of imagination and being imaginative. He describes the criteria of imagination as "unusualness and effectiveness." He gives many examples of people, such as Beethoven, Einstein, and Michelangelo, who are called "imaginative" and shows how their imaginations have manifested themselves. He further argues that it is desirable to develop students' imaginations in order that they too may be able to come up with effective and novel insights and solutions. "I would argue that an educated person, as distinct from a well-trained person or an indoctrinated person, must necessarily possess imagination" (Barrow 1988, p. 89). He says that in order to develop the imagination in students we must encourage their ability to understand. Understanding is not an isolated entity, but is something achieved within particular contexts. There is only understanding of something. He is rather vague on the points or steps that he delineates to develop students' imagination, but one thing he points out is "it would seem reasonable to believe in the importance of widening the experience of the child, both actually and vicariously, and of stimulating the child to attempt an imaginative treatment of material" (Barrow 1988, p. 89). He reminds us that the development of the imagination goes across the curriculum and that teacher modeling and encouragement might be the best approach toward promoting students' imagination.

Michael Degenhardt and Elaine McKay's (1988) main message is that the use of imagination is an important factor in all facets of education and in particular regarding "intercultural understanding," which is defined as similar to the colloquial meaning of social studies. Besides iterating the nature and value of imagination, they delineate ways to foster students' imagination, particularly in reference to issues involving other cultures past and present. One such way to "set the imagination to work" is by "asking pupils to transport themselves to other times and places, perhaps using limited clues and intimations to build up, rich concrete images" (Degenhardt and McKay 1988, p. 237). They admonish educational theorists, who espouse a "commitment to imaginative development," for not coming up with different exercises and ways to develop and nurture imagination in students. They feel that this is easiest to do in reference with particular contexts, hence they offer ideas for "intercultural understanding." "Teaching strategies must be varied, must encourage sympathetic imagination or empathy, and sympathetic re-enactment, and must leave time for reflection and the development of individual responses" (Degenhardt and McKay 1988, pp. 249-250). Some of the varied teaching strategies they suggest are dramatization, first-person writing and examining the art works and artifacts of the culture to promote the "re-enactive imagination" of students. They argue that "imagination is necessary in order to grasp what it is like to see things as they are seen in another culture, to understand another perspective as well as another situation" (Degenhardt and McKay 1988, p. 251).

There has been much research on imagery in general. One of the more recent compilations of such works, which is directly related to teaching, is *Imagery In Education*, edited by Anees A. Sheikh and Katharina S. Sheikh (1985). Most of the studies in this book allude to the efficacious nature of educational methods using imagery. Two of the chapters deal directly with promoting imaging with students. In "The Enhancement of Imaging Ability," the authors cite research that agrees "that everyone has the capacity to image" (Sheikh, Sheikh and Moleski 1985, p. 223). They offer well-researched methods for improving this capacity. Some of these methods include relaxation, concentration, sensory training and direct practice in imaging through particular exercises or fantasy and play.

Within the same book, Beverly-Colleene Galyean (1985) in "Guided Imagery in Education," refers to a variety of studies regarding visualization and guided imagery techniques in elementary and secondary schools as well as colleges and universities. Many of the studies cited are from the "affective/holistic education" literature from the mid 1960s. "Guided cognitive imagery" is used to teach basic subject matter. "Guided affective imagery" is used to increase inner awareness of feelings of self and others. Galyean breaks down the implementation of guided imagery into six steps: 1) relaxing/centering, 2) focusing, 3) multisensing, 4) imaging, 5) communicating and 6) reflecting/interpreting (Galyean 1985, p. 166). Thus, students are asked to take a comfortable position and typically close their eyes and breathe deeply. Once relaxed, students are directed to sharpen their perception in various ways such as to picture a circle, make it a different color and change the shape into a square. The students would then be prompted to mentally experience sensations of seeing, feeling, touching, hearing, tasting and smelling things without those things actually present. The fourth step takes students for "longer imagery journeys which take them to various places, involve them in new situations, and bring them in contact with different people and objects" (Galyean 1985, p. 166). After such an imaginary journey, students are asked to share what happened during the experience. The teacher and other students join with the teller for interpretation and reflection.

It is obviously beyond the scope of this chapter to peruse all of the available literature on enhancing imagination in students. However, little research exists regarding enhancing students' intuitive capacities. Nel Noddings and Paul J. Shore (1984) begin to fill this gap in their comprehensive book, *Awakening the Inner Eye: Intuition in Education*. The authors explore intuition in historical and colloquial contexts. They investigate recent interest in intuition and suggest "intuitive arrangements" for the manner of presentation of subject matter in the curriculum. Noddings and Shore also inquire into the relationship between intuition and love in education. One chapter is devoted to "enhancing intuitive modes" in students. The main emphasis is on intellectual uses of intuition, however, the authors assert that since intuition is so tied to feelings and emotions, enhancing students' intuition necessarily involves some affective translation. They suggest "warming-up exercises" to reduce stress and strain. They mention that "schools cannot provide supportive environments for deeply intuitive modes" (Noddings and Shore 1984, p. 95), but through discussion students can find methods which best enhance their own intuitive capacities. Noddings and Shore emphasize the need for discussion of adult intuition and highly regard the use of biographies and accounts of intuitive occurrences in real-life situations. They suggest that some routinization of the daily activities in the classroom helps students focus on the "objects of knowledge" without having to be distracted by the mechanics of the situation, thus freeing them to be more intuitive. Noddings and Shore suggest that teachers "encourage receptivity" towards intuitive understandings. One way to do this is to avoid too much teacher-directed instruction and allow students opportunity for their own exploration. It is also necessary "to help students maintain the productive tension between subjective certainty and objective uncertainty" (Noddings and Shore 1984, p. 113). To do this teachers are urged to be interested in what the students are trying to accomplish and to keep students convinced that this "uncertainty" always exists. Noddings and Shore suggest that teachers emphasize the students' role of what they should do in a situation rather than an over emphasis on examining what is present.

How do you encourage your students to use their intuitions? Does it make sense to teach students to be more intuitive? How do you foster their imaginations? Do you value imaginative responses from your students?

CHAPTER 10

IMPLICATIONS
AND FURTHER REFLECTION

O World, thou choosest not the better part!
It is not wisdom to be only wise,
And on the inward vision close the eyes,
But it is wisdom to believe the heart.

—George Santayana from
O World, Thou Choosest Not (1894)

Is teachers' everyday use of imagination and intuition a worthwhile endeavor? I find them to be vital elements of the daily commitment teachers make to the perfection of their art. Education is stilted without the application of the teacher's imagination and intuition. All of the exemplary teachers I interviewed and observed in reference to this inquiry view the use of imagination and intuition as essential aspects of daily teaching. The teachers' use of imagination and intuition is crucial to meaningful curricular decision-making and planning. Teachers use imagination and intuition when matching instruction to content and to individual students in day to day practice. Imagination and intuition are highly valued by many quality teachers. Indeed, it has been voiced that education is nonexistent without the use of imagination and intuition.

Egan and Nadaner (1988) recognize that there is no education without the use of the imagination. They view imagination as a fundamental element for any teaching/learning circumstance. They are convinced:

> that imagination is not some desirable but dispensable frill, but that it is the heart of any truly educational experience; it is not something split off from "the basics" or disciplined thought or rational inquiry, but is the quality that can give them life and meaning; it is not something belonging properly to the arts, but is central to all areas of the curriculum; it is not something to ornament our recreational hours, but it is the pragmatic center of all effective human thinking. Our concern is not to promote imagination at the expense of something else—say, rational inquiry or the foundational "3 Rs"; rather it is to show that any conception of rational inquiry or the foundations of education that depreciates imagination is impoverished and sure to be a practical failure. Stimulating the imagination is not an alternative educational activity to be argued for in competition with other claims; it is a prerequisite to making any activity educational. (Egan and Nadaner 1988, p. ix)

It is the teacher's imagination and intuition which breathes life into curricular content, thus making any significant learning possible. The subject matter "comes alive" through imaginative teaching. Students consequently experience this living curriculum in all its excitement. It is during this everyday life of the content, that teachers rely on their intuition to help direct and encourage students. Intuitive thinking is instantaneous. Rubin (1985, p. 60) says that "intuition is of great significance in teaching" due to its interactive nature. He says that "intuition is essential in teaching" (p. 61) because quick assessments and evaluations are constantly demanded of the teacher. No matter how much we come to rely on standardized testing and other normative kinds of assessments, teachers will always need to utilize their own insights for immediate appraisal of students and situations due to the ambiguous nature of personal discourse and general classroom events. The teachers' use of imagination and intuition is valued, not just as a superfluous amenity, but as an *essential* aspect of educational endeavors.

If teachers' imagination and intuition are worthwhile in your estimation it is important to promote their usage not only in your classroom but within your school community as well. We all converse with colleagues regarding students and events occurring in each other's classes. We need to applaud imaginative endeavors and support intuitive behavior whenever possible. It is important to include administrators in such conversations to promote appreciation of teachers' use of imagination and intuition in their classrooms.

Teacher education programs have a basic responsibility for promoting the use of imagination and intuition in education. In order for this to happen, it is necessary for colleges of education to value the use of imagination and intuition on the part of the teacher. This is not always the case. Just as enhancement of teachers' use of imagination and intuition in the schools is made possible through valuation by administrators, promoting such modes in student teachers will only take place in education schools where the use of imagination and intuition are thought to be worthwhile. Rubin (1985, p. 170) has suggested that "Teacher preparation must do everything possible to rekindle idealism and to restore the glory of the mission."

Teaching is indeed a glorious mission. We have chosen for our calling the responsibility for helping to shape the minds and hearts of tomorrow's children, the very future itself. Sometimes our profession is not as highly regarded in the rest of society as it ought to be and this can have an effect on how one views the general worth of one's accomplishments in day to day classroom ventures. We must first and foremost value our own teaching endeavors and those of our colleagues before we can expect others to take notice. The glory we get in teaching most often comes from our students. They will let you know just how worthwhile your use of imagination and intuition is.

Instilling the value of the use of the imagination and intuition promotes putting them into action. When administrators and other authority figures obviously value imaginative and intuitive teaching, teachers feel secure and confident to proceed in this manner in daily activities. It is important for all who value the use of imagination and intuition in education to promote their use in whatever way possible. Idealistic thinking is sorely needed in the profession today. It is only the imaginative person who can be idealistic "to look at things as if they truly could be otherwise" (Greene 1988, p. 55).

How worthwhile are imagination and intuition to you?

Can the "system" work as is to foster imagination and intuition? Concurrent with the acknowledgment of the worthwhile contribution of the imagination and intuition, is the recognition that many educators view the use of imagination and intuition as the antithesis to their educational aim. Such educators have been termed "ignorant" by some teachers I spoke with. Indeed they are unenlightened or "in the dark" as they march decidedly backward fostering ennui. There is a necessity to educate, to enlighten, to "lead from darkness into light" many of those who profess to be educators themselves.

Wertheimer (1945) refers to an intuitive-like experience as "seeing the light." Indeed "enlightenment" often occurs in an intuitive mode. We are reminded of Einstein's insights and valuable intuitions and his total lack of regard for schooling in general and might conclude that such personal, inspirational knowledge has no place in today's back-to-basics schools. In fact, Noddings and Shore (1984, p. 94) tell us that "clearly, schools, with their emphasis on classes and group activities, provide a poor environment for engagement in intuitive modes." The present structure of much of schooling dampens intuitive understandings in students and hampers the teacher's ability to carry out certain imaginative lessons when thought of spontaneously through intuitive receptivity. Teachers are not allowed to react as spontaneously as they might like due to the restrictions and present conventions of many schools.

Albert Einstein once said, "It is in fact nothing short of a miracle that the modern methods of instruction have not entirely strangled the holy curiosity of learning" (Leonard 1968, p. 231). Einstein was dull and unresponsive in school. He was not at all receptive to the methods used. Once his parents enrolled him in a Pestalozzian school, Einstein's progress improved dramatically. As it turns out he was a truly intuitive thinker. The ideas for his major theories came to him in the form of sudden insights through the use of visualization and imagination (Wertheimer 1945). Einstein's commentary is unfortunately still applicable in many schools today.

It is encouraging to have worked with teachers who genuinely value the use of imagination and intuition in teaching, who in fact, cannot fathom teaching without such attributes. Yet, even these teachers who totally espouse these qualities, are quick to realize that imagination and intuition are not universally thought of as worthwhile in schools.

When administrators feel compelled to stress test taking skills and other non-imaginative elements of schooling, teachers are naturally inhibited from displaying imagination and creativity. Certainly if they are encouraged to direct students to learn that there is only one right answer, teachers will be stifling the openness needed for intuitive understanding and the creative spark. This overemphasis on raising test scores keeps teaching on a low plane of involvement. It stimulates the teacher to think in terms of having all of the answers. It suggests that students need to be *told* rather than to be encouraged to *discover*. It discourages any higher order of creative thinking. It urges teachers to employ the text-book/ditto master approach to "teaching." And, besides, it is extremely dull and boring for all concerned.

It is the belief that there is only one correct way to do something that leads to unimaginative teaching and, therefore, a lack of learning and understanding. This is what has been happening in many classrooms due to the emphasis on standardized tests, which look for one correct response. The focus on multiple choice tests is destroying teaching students to think for themselves. If one is always teaching towards better test scores, then there is little room for any real learning to occur. There is minimal room for discovery.

It is an interesting dilemma. As an administrator, I have always told teachers that these tests have little value and that they must trust their own insights as professionals. In general I have promoted imaginative and intuitive teaching. However, each year when evalua-tion reports need to be compiled based on the annual standardized test scores, I find myself along with every-body else engrossed in the interpretation of these num-bers as if they represented some magical solution to all educational problems. Often when consulting with teach-ers about particular students, test scores will be referred to as some blueprint of understanding the inner work-ings of the individual. I find myself looking at them and trying to make some sense of the distorted picture they create. I have witnessed administrators downplay the importance of the tests, only to have the scores finally confront them on some level so as to alter their stance in this regard.

To test or not to test does not seem to be the question at hand. Rather it seems that testing with all its problems is an inevitable reality at this time. Some states are seriously looking into the need for more humane assessment. Tests with more than one right answer are given to students so that they must choose the two or three correct solutions out of five or six possibilities. This may be a step in the right direction, however small it might seem. Writing assessments are required by many states. Students are given a topic and told to compose an essay response which is then read in its entirety by several trained evaluators who arrive at a holistic numerical score. Indeed test makers are being required to come up with alternative forms of assessment. Unfortunately most of these assessments try to remove the teacher from the evaluation process. I believe we need to look to teachers as instruments of assessments and accept their insights regarding the students we have entrusted to them.

Maxine Greene (1978, 1981, 1988) depicts imagination and intuition as fundamental components of education. However, she is recently concerned that the educational reports of the late 1980s, calling for reform, have overlooked the use of the imagination. She says that the use of imagination, the noncognitive and the intuitive are all identified "with the merely playful; and none of these are granted relevance for serious learning or for mastery" (Greene 1988, p. 45). This lack of openness to "alternative possibilities" is bothering to her. This manner of thinking gives rise to routinization and boredom in teaching. If education is to lead us down the tedious path of ennui, reformation has indeed turned to deformation. This is a backwards journey into darkness, into the abyss of ignorance. Greene (1988, p. 48) advocates the use of imagination as she looks toward "a kind of education that recognizes imagination as fundamental to learning to learn, essential to the feeling that life is more than a futile, repetitive, consuming exercise."

How do you see imagination and intuition working within your school system?

Why are not more educators striving to be more imaginative and intuitive? It is understandable why so many "unenlightened" educators are not straying from the path of routinization and boredom—there is simply too much effort involved with *true* reform, with restructuring the process of schooling. It is easier to urge the addition of similar structure, to advocate particular frameworks and systematized ways of looking at things. An imaginative, intuitive manner of teaching calls for investment of time and effort. The unfortunate scenario in many schools is a drive toward efficiency with little regard for quality. This affords little knowledge to the students as we slip backwards toward the darkness of the abyss, lacking in the true meaning of *educare.* Although efficiency and efficacy need not be mutually exclusive, it is necessary to invest time and energy into our endeavors to make them worthwhile. This need for hurried and often careless instruction in schools is reflective of our society in general. We have a tendency to look for the short cuts in many things we do, but often the longer more scenic route actually seems to take less time because it is so enjoyable.

> *The times have taken a fearsome toll on the raw edge of despair. Disillusioned and embittered, they no longer care. There was a day—a day that must be returned—when individuals with great gifts thought the teaching of children a worthy lifetime endeavor. It still is.*

—Louis Rubin (1985, p. 170)

The school community certainly is a reflection of the mood of society in general. We have become a fast paced, somewhat embittered and indifferent populace in general. These attributes are antithetical to the use of the imagination and intuition. Imaginative teaching takes more time and involvement on the part of the teacher than merely following the teacher guide and complying with mandated instruction. It takes a thoughtful, sensitive person to teach in an imaginative and intuitive manner.

Since schooling is so much a part of our indoctrination into society, it is no wonder that there are many educators who have come from unimaginative institutions ready and willing to carry on the standards they have come to respect in schools. "If it was good enough for me . . . This is the way I was taught . . ." Certainly we have all heard teachers voice such phrases. If one is taught that there is one correct way to do something rather than to discover all the possible ways of doing it, it seems obvious that one ought to continue doing it the "right" way. If knowledge is always parcelled out into specific subject areas and time blocks for us, it is difficult to envision learning in a less regimented fashion. Schools reflect society and society reflects schooling.

Why do you think some educators do not value imagination and intuition?

Why can't schools be fun? The use of imagination and intuition is an avenue toward enjoyment in school learning situations. It is the teachers' daily use of imagination and intuition that encourages students to exercise these modes of thought and knowledge access. The more students are allowed to be imaginative and intuitive, the faster that they will learn and the more they will enjoy the learning process. It is fun to learn. There is great satisfaction inherently involved with learning. It is up to the teacher to recognize this and encourage fun in imaginative learning.

We need to reconsider our idea of what schools should be to encourage the use of the imagination and intuition. The classroom milieu ought to be designed to foster interaction, spontaneity and openness. It would be welcome to embrace the idea of randomness and play in the school environment. We need a more naturally balanced approach to the elements of structure and randomness. We need to be more open to variety in terms of activities and approaches to teaching and learning. Teachers need to look at all the possibilities afforded to them and to the students. Looking at things in new ways and discovery in general are enjoyable activities—they are fun! Imaginative ideas for lessons are a necessity in order for students to connect with the material, each other and the teacher. We must strive for "imaginative fullness" to elucidate the context for genuine comprehension. With our assistance we can have confidence that the students will intuitively realize their own enlightenment. What amazing joy—what fun it is to learn!

The teacher's job as facilitater is to "lead." Teachers need to show students how to take learning on their own terms. Learning is a personal endeavor on the part of the student that is facilitated by the teacher. Enlightenment takes place through the "conversation" of teaching. The creative spark is ignited. Where there is a spark there can be a fire. To educate is to lead from darkness into light—if there is no spark, you are still in the darkness it is dull and joyless. Once you kindle the spark, then you can see in order to lead out. The teacher and the students fan the fire together. The blaze gets brighter and brighter as students "see the light" of understanding. How can you help but have a good time when you are doing such an exciting thing as teaching and learning?

Do your students enjoy learning with you?

What do we need for imaginative, intuitive teaching? We need to better articulate the concepts of imagination and intuition. More insightful language is needed to help legitimize and foster teachers' use of imagination and intuition. The language developed in Parts II and III of this book is an example of such useful articulation. The unraveling of the "threads" in Part III is a worthwhile process for this purpose. The more we are able to share with each other in this regard, the more we will be able to encourage imaginative and intuitive teaching in general.

The ideas discussed in chapter 8 of this part of the book add to this needed rhetoric. On an individual level, self assessment, reading and reflecting are all necessary to aid oneself in continuing to teach in an imaginative and intuitive fashion. Sharing with colleagues serves all involved. The more we familiarize ourself with and deliberate the issues, the more they become a natural part of our day to day teaching repertoire. It is necessary for those who value imaginative and intuitive teaching as worthwhile endeavors to encourage others to teach with similar zeal.

Commitment, time, and effort are essential components for imaginative, intuitive teaching. The emotional commitment associated with teaching in an imaginative and intuitive way is tiring yet always exhilarating and fulfilling. As one teacher pointed out, in good teaching "caring is the bottom line." In my first administrative job in an elementary school in the mid 1970s, I remember coming to a similar conclusion—student comprehension did not depend on specific techniques and methods. A concerned, caring teacher is all that *actually* matters for any classroom situation to be considered outstanding. Genuine caring in teaching manifests itself as imaginative and intuitive. Noddings and Shore (1984, p. 175) tell us that

A caring, concerned teacher should be aware of the intuitive factors shaping student perceptions of subject matter. Likewise, as educators become more aware of the role of intuition in interpersonal relations, they will come to value caring and educational caritas even more than before. If we remain open to the possibility of expanding and strengthening the use of intuition and the expression of caring, then education can be a more meaningful experience for both student and teacher. Beyond this, the legitimization by schools of such generally deemphasized topics as love and intuition will aid their more widespread acceptance by the public and will earn these human capabilities a greater place in our conception of the functioning, thinking feeling human being.

When we truly care, our concern and emotional commitment to the students, subject matter and the classroom milieu enable us to educate in the true sense of the word. Teachers' everyday use of imagination and intuition is imperative for *educare*, sincere teaching. "Genuine education, leading from darkness to light, is accomplished with the brilliant flame of intuition, the passionate blaze of imagination, the luminous kindling of caring and the radiant glow of love" (Jagla 1992, p. 78).

What do we need for imaginative, intuitive teaching? We need you! It is up to individual teachers to make a difference. We are powerful figures in the lives of our students. Sometimes we forget what power and influence we really possess. Within the domain of our own classrooms the possibilities are infinite as long as we remain open to our own imagination and intuition.

REFERENCES

Arnheim, R. (1985). The double-edged mind: Intuition and the intellect. In E.W. Eisner (Ed.), *Learning and teaching, The ways of knowing.* Eighty-fourth yearbook of the National Society for the Study of Education, Part II. Chicago: University of Chicago Press, 77-96.

Barell, J. (1980). *Playgrounds of our minds.* New York: Teachers College Press.

Barrow, R. (1988). Some observations on the concept of imagination. In Egan, K. and D. Nadaner (Eds.), *Imagination and education.* New York: Teachers College Press, 79-90.

Berne, E. (1977). *Intuition and ego states: The origins of transactional analysis.* San Francisco: TA Press.

Blom, J.J. (1977). *Rules for the direction of the mind.* (translation of René Descartes). New York: New York University Press.

Bloom, B.S. (1956). *Taxonomy of educational objectives: Handbook I, Cognitive domain.* New York: David McKay Co., Inc.

Bronowski, J. (1971). *The identity of man.* New York: Natural History Press.

Brophy, J.E., and M.M. Rohrkemper. (1981). The influence of problem ownership on teachers' perception of and strategies for coping with problem students. *Journal of educational psychology*, 73, 295-311.

Bruner, J. (1978). *The process of education*. Cambridge, MA.: Harvard University Press.

Carson, T. (1986). Closing the gap between research and practice: Conversation as a mode of doing research. *Phenomenology and pedagogy*, 4(2), 73-85.

Clandinin, D.J. (1986). *Classroom practice, Teacher images in action*. London: The Falmer Press.

Clark, C.M., and P.L. Peterson. (1986). Teachers' thought processes. In M.C. Wittrock (Ed.), *Handbook of research on teaching*. New York: Macmillan, 255-296.

Coleridge, S.T. (1817). *Biographia Literaria*. J. Shawcross (Ed.). Oxford: Oxford University Press, 1907.

Connelly, F.M. and M. Ben-Peretz. (1980). Teachers' roles in the using and doing of research and curriculum development. *Journal of curriculum studies*, 12, 95-107.

Connelly, F.M., and D.J. Clandinin. (1985). Narrative history and the study of minded practice. A paper presented at the Meadow Brook Conference on Collborative Action Research, Oakland University, Rochester, MI, January 20-23, 1985.

Degenhardt, M., and E. McKay. (1988). Imagination and education for intercultural understanding. In Egan, K. and D. Nadaner (Eds.), *Imagination and education*. New York: Teachers College Press, 237-255.

De Mille, R. (1976). *Put your mother on the ceiling*. New York: Penguin Books.

Dewey, J. (1900). *The school and society*. Chicago: University of Chicago Press.

Dewey, J. (1902). *The child and the curriculum*. Chicago: University of Chicago Press.

Dewey, J. (1910). *How we think.* Lexington, MA.: D. C. Heath.

Dewey, J. (1916). *Democracy and education.* New York: Macmillan.

Dewey, J. (1938). *Experience and education.* New York: Macmillan.

Doyle, W. (1986). Classroom organization and management. In M.C. Wittrock (Ed.), *Handbook of research on teaching.* New York: Macmillan, 392-431.

Edwards, K.C. (1966). *The Dewey school.* New York: Atheneum.

Egan, K. (1986). *Teaching as storytelling: An alternative approach to teaching and curriculum in the elementary school.* London, Ontario: The Althouse Press.

Egan, K. (1988a). The origins of the imagination and the curriculum. In Egan, K. and D. Nadaner (Eds.), *Imagination and education.* New York: Teachers College Press, 91-127.

Egan, K. (1988b). Memory and story in teacher's knowledge and action. A paper presented at the annual meeting of the American Educational research Association in New Orleans Louisiana.

Egan, K., and D. Nadaner (Eds.). (1988). *Imagination and education.* New York: Teachers College Press.

Eisner, E.W. (1983). The art and craft of teaching. *Educational leadership,* 40(4), 4-13.

Eisner, E.W. (1985a). *The educational imagination, On the design and evaluation of school programs.* New York: Macmillan.

Eisner, E.W. (Ed.). (1985b). *Learning and teaching the ways of knowing.* Eighty-fourth yearbook of the national society for the study of education, Part II. Chicago: University of Chicago Press.

Elbaz, F.L. (1983). *Teacher thinking: A study of practical knowledge.* London: Croom Helm.

Fehmi, L. (1975). Open focus training. Paper presented at the Council Grove Conference on Voluntary Control of Internal States on April 3rd. Council Grove, Kansas: The Menninger Foundation. Feitelson, D. and G.S. Ross (1973). The neglected factor—play. In *Human development*, 16, 202-223.

Feldhusen, J.F., D.J. Treffinger, and S.J. Bahlke. (1970). Developing creative thinking: The Purdue creativity program. *Journal of creative behavior*, 4, 85-90.

Finch, M.E. (1978). *Behind the teacher's desk: A study of the teacher and the change process*. Doctoral dissertation, Washington University.

Freyberg, J.T. (1973). Increasing the imaginative play of urban disadvantaged kindergarten children through systematic training. In *The child's world of make-believe*, J. Singer (Ed.). New York: Academic Press.

Galyean, B.C. (1985). Guided imagery in education. In *Imagery in education*, A.A. Sheikh and K.S. Sheikh (Eds.). Farmingdale, New York: Baywood Publishing Company, Inc., 161-177.

Garcia, E. (1987). An ethnographic study of teachers' implicit theories on evaluation. A paper presented at the annual meeting of the American Educational Research Association in Washington, D.C.

Garfinkel, H. (1977). What is ethnomethodology? In F.R. Dalmayr and T.A. McCarthy (Eds.), *Understanding and social inquiry*. Notre Dame: University of Notre Dame Press, 240-261.

Goodlad, J.I., and M.F. Klein. (1970). *Behind the classroom door*. Worthingtom, OH: Charles A. Jones.

Goodman, Y.M. (1985). Kidwatching: Observing children in the classroom. In *Observing the language learner*, A. Jaggar and M.T. Smith-Burke (Eds.). Newark, DE.: International Association of Reading, 9-18.

Gottlieb, S. (1973). Modeling effects upon fantasy. In *The child's world of make-believe*, J. Singer (Ed.). New York: Academic Press.

Greene, J.L., and R. Weade. (1988). Teaching as conversation and the construction of meaning in the classroom. A paper presented at annual meeting of American Educational Research Association in New Orleans, Louisiana.

Greene, M. (1973). *Teacher as stranger.* New York: Wadsworth.

Greene, M. (1978). *Landscapes of learning.* New York: Teachers College Press.

Greene, M. (1981). Educational research and the arts: A dialogue with Elliot Eisner and Maxine Greene. A symposium presented at the 1981 Annual Meeting of the American Educational Research Association. Los Angeles.

Greene, M. (1988). What happened to imagination? In Egan, K. and D. Nadaner (Eds.), *Imagination and education.* New York: Teachers College Press, 45-56.

Griffing, P. (1974). Sociodramatic play among young black children. In *Theory into practice*, 13, 257-264.

Griffiths, R. (1935). *A study of imagination in early childhood.* London: Kegan Paul, Trench, Trubner.

Haley-Oliphant, A.E. (1987). Teacher thinking-in-action regarding the use of hypothetical questions in a science classroom. A paper presented at the annual meeting of the American Educational Research Association in Washington, D.C.

Hansen, K. (1988). Education and the perceptive imagination. In Egan, K. and D. Nadaner (Eds.), *Imagination and education.* New York: Teachers College Press, 128-149.

Hohler, T.P. (1982). *Imagination and reflection: Intersubjectivity.* Boston: The Hague/Martinus & Nijhoff.

Hughes, T. (1988). Myth and education. In Egan, K. and D. Nadaner (Eds.), *Imagination and education.* New York: Teachers College Press, 30-44.

Hunter, E. (1972). *Encounter in the classroom.* New York: Holt, Rinehart and Winston.

Jackson, P.W. (1968). *Life in classrooms.* New York: Holt, Rinehart, and Winston.

Jagla, V.M. (1989). *In pursuit of the elusive image: An inquiry into teachers' everyday use of imagination and intuition.* Doctoral dissertation. Chicago: University of Illinois.

Jagla, V.M. (1990). In pursuit of the elusive image: An inquiry into teachers' everyday use of imagination and intuition. *Kappa Delta Pi Record,* 26(4): 106-110.

Jagla, V.M. (1992). Teachers' everyday imagination and intuition. In *Teacher lore: Learning from our own experience.* W. H. Schubert and W. C. Ayers (Eds.). New York: Longman, 61-79.

Janesick, V. (1982). Of snakes and circles: Making sense of classroom group processes through a case study. *Curriculum inquiry,* 12(2), 161-190.

Jung, C.G. (1923). *Psychological Types.* New York: Pantheon Press.

Kant, I. (1781, 1787). *Critique of pure reason.* New York: St. Martin's Press, 1970.

Kneller, G.F. (1984). *Movements of thought in modern education.* New York: John Wiley and Sons.

Leonard, G. (1968). *Education and ecstasy.* New York: Delacorte.

Lincoln, Y.S., and E.G. Guba. (1985). *Naturalistic inquiry.* Beverly Hills, CA.: Sage.

Marcelo, C. (1987). A study of implicit theories and beliefs about teaching in elementary school teachers. A paper presented at the annual meeting of the American Educational Research Association in Washington, D.C.

Matthews, G. (1988). The philosophical imagination in children's literature. In Egan, K. and D. Nadaner (Eds.), *Imagination and education.* New York: Teachers College Press, 186-197.

Meyers, R.E., and E.P. Torrance. (1965). *Ideabooks* (five titles). Lexington, MA.: Ginn and Company.

Noddings, N. (1984). *Caring: A feminine approach to ethics and moral education.* Berkley: University of California Press.

Noddings, N., and P.J. Shore. (1984). *Awakening the inner eye, Intuition in education.* New York: Teachers College Press.

Oakeshott, M. (1959). *Poetry and the conversation of mankind.* London: Bowes and Bowes.

Planck, M. (1933). *Where is science going?* (J. Murphy, trans.). London: Allen and Unwin.

Polanyi, M. (1962). *Personal Knowledge.* Chicago: The University of Chicago Press.

Richards, J.C., and J.P. Gipe. (1988). Reflective thinking and the teaching abilities of prospective teachers. A paper presented at the annual meeting of the American Educational Research Association in New Orleans, Louisiana.

Richert, A.E. (1987). Reflection and pedagogical caring: Unsilencing the teacher's voice. A paper presented at the annual meeting of the American Educational Research Association in Washington, D.C.

Rosen, C.E. (1974). The effects of sociodramatic play on problem-solving behavior among culturally disadvantaged preschool children. In *Child development,* 45, 920-927.

Rubin, L.J. (1985). *Artistry in teaching.* New York: Random House.

Rugg, H. (1963). *Imagination.* New York: Harper and Row.

Russell, T., and P. Johnston. (1988). Teachers learning from experiences of teaching: Analyses based on metaphor and reflection. A paper presented at the annual meeting of the American Educational Research Association in New Orleans, Louisiana.

Ryle, G. (1949). *The concept of mind.* London: Hutchinson.

Saltz, E., D. Dixon, and J. Johnson. (1977). Training disadvantaged preschoolers on various fantasy activities: Effects on cognitive functioning and impulse control. In *Child development*, 48, 367-380

Saltz, E., and J. Johnson. (1974). Training for thematic-fantasy play in culturally disadvantaged children: Preliminary results. In *Journal of educational psychology*, 66 (4), 623-630.

Sartre, J.P. (1948). *The psychology of imagination*. New York: Philosophical Library.

Schon, D. (1983). *The reflective practitioner*. New York: Basic Books.

Schubert, W.H. (1975). *Imaginative projection: A method of curriculum invention*. Doctoral dissertation, University of Illinois at Champaign-Urbana.

Schubert, W.H. (1986). *Curriculum: Perspective, paradigm, and possibility*. New York: Macmillan Publishing Company.

Schwab, J.J. (1969). The practical: A language for curriculum. *School Review*, 78, 1-23.

Schwab, J.J. (1970). *The practical: A language for curriculum*. Washington, D.C.: National Education Association.

Schwab, J.J. (1971). The practical: Arts of eclectic. *School Review*, 79, 493-542.

Schwab, J.J. (1973). The practical 3: Translation into curriculum. *School Review*, 81,501-522.

Seidman, I.E., and S.A. Santilli. (1988). In-depth phenomenological interviewing: A qualitative approach to understanding the experience of beginning teachers. A paper presented at the annual meeting of the American Educational Research Association in New Orleans, Louisiana.

Sheikh, A.A., and K.S. Sheikh. (1985). *Imagery in education*, Farmingdale, New York: Baywood Publishing Company.

Sheikh, A.A., K.S. Sheikh, and L.M. Moleski. (1985). The enhancement of imaging ability. In *Imagery in educa-*

tion, A.A. Sheikh and K.S. Sheikh (Eds.). Farmingdale, New York: Baywood Publishing Company, Inc., 223-239.

Sinatra, R., and J. Stahl-Gemake. (1983). *Using the right brain in the language arts*. Springfield, Illinois: Charles C. Thomas, Publisher.

Singer, J.L. (1973). *The child's world of make-believe*. New York: Academic Press.

Singer, J.L., and D.G. Singer. (1976). Imaginative play and pretending: Some experimental approaches. In *Child personality and Psychopathology*, A. Davids (Ed.). New York: Wiley.

Smilansky, S. (1973). *The effects of socio-dramatic play on disadvantaged preschool children*. New York: Wiley.

Smith, J.A. (1966). *Setting conditions for creative teaching in the elementary school*. Boston: Allyn and Bacon.

Smith, P.K., M. Dagleish, and G. Herzmark. (1981). A comparison of the effects of fantasy play tutoring and skills tutoring in nursery classes. In *International journal of behavioral development*, 4, 42-1441.

Smith, P.K. and S. Sydall. (1978). Play and non-play tutoring in pre-school children: Is it play or tutoring which matters. In *British journal of educational psychology*, 48, 315-325.

Sturrock, J. (1988). How the graminivorous ruminating quadruped jumped over the moon: A romantic approach. In Egan, K. and D. Nadaner (Eds.), *Imagination and education*. New York: Teachers College Press, 57-75.

Sutherland, M.B. (1971). *Everyday imagining and education*. London: Routledge and Kegan Paul.

Torrance, E.P. (1964). *Education and the creative potential*. Minneapolis: The University of Minnesota Press.

Torrance, E.P. (1977). *Creativity in the classroom*. Washington, D.C.: National Education Association.

Torrance, E.P. (1981). Creative teaching makes a difference. In J.C. Gowan, J. Khatena, and E.P. Torrance (Eds.), *Creativity: Its educational implications.* Dubuque, IA.: Kendall/Hunt Publishing Company.

Torrance, E.P., and J.P. Torrance. (1973). *Is creativity teachable?* Bloomington, IN.: Phi Delta Kappa Educational Foundation.

Torrance, E.P., and R.E. Meyers. (1970). *Creative learning and teaching.* New York: Dodd, Mead and Company.

Udwin, O., and D. Shmuckler. (1981). The influences of sociocultural, economic and home background factors on children's ability to engage in imaginative play. In *Developmental psychology,* 17:1, pp. 66-72.

van Manen, M. (1984). Practicing phenomenological writing. *Phenomenology and pedagogy,* 2(1), 36-69.

Vaughan, F.E. (1979). *Awakening intuition.* Garden City, NY.: Anchor/Doubleday.

Webster's ninth new collegiate dictionary. (1987). Springfield, Massachusetts: Merriam-Webster, Inc.

Weininger, O. (1988). "What if" and "as if": Imagination and pretend play in early childhood. In Egan, K. and D. Nadaner (Eds.), *Imagination and education.* New York: Teachers College Press, 141-149.

Wertheimer, M. (1945). *Productive thinking.* New York: Harper and Row.

INDEX